"Praise for Cooperstown

"Anyone even remotely interested in baseball is apt to become enraptured with the Baseball Hall of Fame after reading Canadian Rudy Gafur's interesting account of his annual pilgrimages to the shrine at Cooperstown, New York.

'Cooperstown is My Mecca' represents a unique tribute to the writers and broadcasters who have been honoured at Cooperstown over the years."
— *Phil Collier, San Diego Union-Tribune*

"Rudy Gafur moved to Canada from Guyana in the seventies. Unlike Julius Caesar, he came, he saw and he fell in love with baseball. Originally, it was with a team which was losing 100 games a season, but his passionate love affair grew to encompass the game, its rich history and the Baseball Hall of Fame. Now the author has conquered. If you're going to Cooperstown take this book with you."
— *Bob Elliott, Baseball Columnist, Toronto Sun*

"Gafur's love for baseball is reflected everywhere in the book. He has captured the art, tradition, history and culture – the very heart and spirit of the National Pastime.

Baseball survives and thrives because of dedicated, loyal fans like Rudy Gafur."
— *Ben Steidman, NCC Publications Ltd., Delhi, Ontario*

"The first thing that struck me . . . was Gafur's enthusiasm. Here is someone stricken with baseball fever who went directly to the source for a cure. He confidently and reverently charges forward in search of his new-found heroes with the carefree devotion . . . you see in kids on a sandlot. Cooperstown . . . is a picturesque tourist spot and Gafur's journey is described in travelogue detail for those who have never been there.

But the book's charm is in his recollections of meeting baseball's greats and their families. Gafur is someone on a pilgrimage who refuses to miss his chance of touching history. A newcomer to the game he proves that, no matter who you are or where you come from, when you catch it, baseball fever is hard to break."
— *David Fuller, Editor-in-Chief, The Scarborough Mirror*

"This book . . . should appeal to those who have an abiding interest in just what happens on Hall of Fame Weekend, or who want to see Cooperstown put in the best possible light.

The text is interspersed with an obvious reverence for the Hall of Fame and descriptive accolades for the players within."

— *Dan Sheridan, Editor, Freeman's Journal, Cooperstown*

"The book radiates with energy and enthusiasm and certainly shows a fan's devotion to the game . . . and to the Baseball Hall of Fame."

— *Terri Johnson, Night Editor, The Daily Star, Oneonta, N.Y.*

"A 'baseball nut' . . . Gafur's unabashed love for the game and his knowledge of its rich history certainly qualify him to write "Cooperstown is My Mecca."

. . . the book provides a wealth of information for prospective visitors and would certainly be a welcome addition to most baseball fans' libraries."

— *Roger Lajoie, Sports Editor, Oshawa This Week,*
Oshawa, Ontario

" 'Cooperstown is My Mecca' . . . is more than just a baseball book. It is a part of literature. If you haven't visited Cooperstown before, you will make your first trip with this book. Rudy puts you in Cooperstown, not just inside the Hall of Fame.

And you thought there was only one memorable line – 'Say it ain't so, Joe' – by a youngster in baseball. Rudy Gafur discovered another . . . that centres around the great Ted Williams. Don't miss it."

— *Jerry Howarth, Broadcaster, Toronto Blue Jays*

". . . . As someone who has never had the opportunity to visit the National Baseball Hall of Fame, I found 'Cooperstown is My Mecca' a wondrous personal insight, brought to me through the author's own experiences and growing affection for the game, all the while in a charmingly folksy style.

Baseball is lucky to have fans like Rudy Gafur, and even more fortunate they have a desire to profess their love of this great game. After reading this book, I feel closer to the game than ever before."

— *Rick Campbell, Publisher, Waterloo (Ontario) Chronicle*

"Written by an outsider who adopted our national game, the book gives fans the ins and outs of the Baseball Hall of Fame and the Induction Ceremonies, and captures the essence of the sleepy little village of Cooperstown. Fans, young and old, will appreciate Gafur's account of his pilgrimage to Baseball's Mecca."

— *Ed Michels, Independent Mirror-Citizen*
Outlet-Phoenix Register

"I thoroughly enjoyed reading Rudy Gafur's book on Cooperstown and the Hall of Fame. He is a man obviously in love with the game of baseball and the shrine that the game reserves for its heroes.

I have never been to the Hall of Fame but after having read this book, I can't wait to make my first trip to Cooperstown. This book is a must read for all baseball fans who treasure the game's great history."

— *Chris Wheeler, Broadcaster, Philadelphia Phillies*

"Mr. Gafur's detailed account of his journeys to Cooperstown is a true gift to baseball and its fans . . . A wonderful tribute to our National Pastime."

— *Dwight Gram III, Rich Publications/Buffalo Bisons Baseball*

COOPERSTOWN IS MY MECCA

by

RUDY A. S. GAFUR

Merrick
Feel the passion
Go the distance
Rudy Gafur
Sun. Aug. 4, 1996

Canadian Cataloguing in Publication Data

Gafur, Rudy A. S., 1941 –
   Cooperstown is my mecca

1st Canadian ed.
Includes bibliographical references and index.
ISBN 0-9699173-0-9

   1. National Baseball Hall of Fame and Museum.
2. Cooperstown (N.Y.).   3. Gafur, Rudy A. S.,
1941 –   .   I. Title.

GV863.A1G34 1995 796.357'074'74774 C95-900117-4

Cover design: Rudy A.S. Gafur and Leo Salvador.

All photographs courtesy of the author.

For information contact:

        NCC Printing and Publishing,
        300 Argyle Avenue,
        Delhi, Ontario
        Canada, N4B 2Y1

CONTENTS

Dedication...i

Introduction...ii

Acknowledgement..iv

Preface v

CHAPTER I. *The Conversion* 1

CHAPTER II. *The First Journey* 5

CHAPTER III. *Gods Among Men*......................................19

CHAPTER IV. *They Started Something Here* 29

CHAPTER V. *The Second Coming* 37

CHAPTER VI. *There's More to Cooperstown* 47

CHAPTER VII. *Wilver and Ken* 55

CHAPTER VIII. *The Anniversaries* 63

CHAPTER IX. *O! Canada*...81

CHAPTER X. *The Terrific Turnout* 95

CHAPTER XI. *The Scribes*...103

CHAPTER XII. *The Broadcasters*.......................................139

EPILOGUE...155

APPENDIX A An Insider's Guide to Cooperstown 159

APPENDIX B Services offered by the National Baseball Library
    and Archive...169

APPENDIX C Criteria for Election to the Hall of Fame 171

APPENDIX D Cooperstown Business District....................................177

APPENDIX E Map of Cooperstown...179

APPENDIX F Route Map to Cooperstown...181

APPENDIX G Parking in Cooperstown..183

APPENDIX H Members of the National Baseball Hall of Fame 185

BIBLIOGRAPHY 189

DEDICATION

This book is dedicated to:

The Present: *Tony Kubek, for his inspiration, friendship and encouragement.*

The Past: *Jim Cobb, whose father's exploits led me to become a devotee of the National Baseball Hall of Fame and Museum.*

The Future: *Dairl John Flood, Jr., who will someday carry the torch and become a better fan than his "Grampa".*

INTRODUCTION

When you've been around any business for over thirty-seven years you can count on meeting a wide variety of people. It's been that way for me during a nine year career as a major league baseball player and the ensuing twenty-eight as a television announcer, twelve of which were spent covering the Blue Jays in Toronto. But how many of those that you meet snap your focus to attention and have that inexplicable, "little something" that attracts and holds like a magnet?

Among the managers whom I've met with "that quality" I'd list "The Ole Perfesser", Casey Stengel, the controversial Leo "The Lip" Durocher and the Baltimore Orioles brilliant leader, Earl Weaver. Some of the players special to me would be the last .400 hitter - "The Splendid Splinter" - Ted Williams; perhaps the most dynamic player ever, Mickey Mantle; the nearly unhittable Sandy Koufax, and baseball's greatest showman of my time, the fabulous Willie Mays; and WOW! I'll never forget the day I met Tyrus Raymond Cobb at an old-timers' day at Yankee Stadium., Then, there are the celebrity fans like former president, Richard M. Nixon or the California Angels' colorful owner, The Singing Cowboy, Gene Autry. If you travel to Boston, you will likely hear about an eccentric "Sox" fanatic; his name is Chuck Waselewski and he has catalogued every baseball hit over or off Fenway's fabled Green Monster in recent recorded history.

There are the irrepressible chroniclers of our game, the wordsmiths like "Red" Smith, the flamboyant Jimmy Cannon and Dick Young who got your attention in a hurry - and kept it. The stentorian voices of Ernie Harwell, Curt Gowdy and Mel Allen rivetted you to an important "at bat" like no one else could; you don't want to take your eyes off the ball when it's headed toward shortstop and Ozzie Smith is there. What unique threads all, interwoven amid the fabric of baseball.

My friend Rudy A. S. Gafur of Agincourt, Ontario, Canada occupies a niche among my unique baseball acquaintances. No, he hasn't contributed noticeably to the lore of the game, not yet, anyway. His background, unlikely as it seems, has aided in molding a dedicated student of "the game" with an insatiable and ardent passion for its history. Like a sponge he has soaked up and stored volumes of baseball anecdotal treasures, some through his research, but mostly through first-hand conversations with many of baseball's greats or their intimate friends or close relatives. He's done this during his many sojourns to baseball's shrine at Cooperstown. On more than one occasion with very little squeezing, Rudy has let loose some of the wonderfully novel stories he has gathered at The Hall and related them to me in a refreshingly captivating manner. His friendship with Ty Cobb's son Jim, and the stories that flow from their friendship are especially poignant.

During my years working or just watching ballgames in either Toronto's antiquated Exhibition Stadium or their new, state of the art, Skydome, I attended over five-hundred ballgames. Seldom can I recall not having seen Rudy at the game, and invariably I found myself hoping our paths would intersect so that I could hurriedly gather a tidbit to pass on to our viewing audience. Seeing Rudy's eyes twinkle and listening to his voice lovingly retell the stories of his baseball adventures is probably the best way to get the message of this true "baseball junkie". On the other hand, he seems to have saved the best for his writing debut in this publication, <u>Cooperstown is my Mecca.</u>

Tony Kubek

Menasha, Wisconsin
September 1994

ACKNOWLEDGEMENT

This book, my first attempt at large-scale writing, was an easy and enjoyable project. My affection for the National Pastime, my fascination with the National Baseball Hall of Fame and the encouragement and support I received, made it an almost effortless exercise. Nevertheless, it could not have become a reality without the contributions of a number of special people. With deep appreciation and heartfelt thanks I acknowledge them: Dave McCuaig of Lever Bros. and Jerry Howarth of the Telemedia Broadcasting Service for their assistance in preparing my application to the Canada Council and for their encouragement; Carole MacKey for research at the Hall of Fame. Bill Deane, former Senior Research Associate of the National Baseball Hall of Fame promptly responded to my request for research material and offered suggestions for improvement. The source of boundless goodwill and inspiration, Tony Kubek, broadcaster and former New York Yankees shortstop, gave unselfishly of his time in writing the Introduction and in urging me on with the project. I would like to acknowledge also, my fellow Hall of Fame pilgrims. Their names are too numerous to list here, but they know who they are.

Thanks too, to my unofficial editors, Dr. Anne Lloyd and her husband David Barnes. We are still friends despite the many changes in the script. Frances Edmonds, Production Co-Ordinator of N.C.C. Printing and Publishing, assisted in designing the cover; my friend Liz Henry, Costing and Estimating Manager, (also of N.C.C.), was an inexhaustible source of advice and assistance on a myriad of matters relating to the publication of the book. My thanks to Frances and Liz also. Finally, my undying gratitude is extended to Gary MacDonald and Alice Ferrier who demonstrated the true meaning of the biblical injunction "Love thy neighbour". Gary endured my long discussions with Alice and acted as a sounding board for some of my ideas. Alice's monumental patience, dedication and work at her computer terminal brought order to my jumbled bits of manuscript.

Take a bow folks.

Agincourt, Ontario
December, 1994

Rudy Gafur

PREFACE

This book is the story of a pilgrimage, a pilgrimage born of a fan's fascination with the National Baseball Hall of Fame and Museum.

Hindus visit the Ganges river; Muslims go to Mecca; baseball devotees visit Cooperstown. The Ganges river is sacred to Hindus so they go to the river to wash and purify their bodies and souls. Muslims make pilgrimage to Mecca because it is the birthplace of their Prophet Muhammad and because they are required to do so by their religion, Islam. The Baseball Hall of Fame in Cooperstown, New York, is the shrine to which baseball fans go to pay homage to their heroes.

Mecca is the most widely-known and highly-regarded of the world's religious shrines. Indeed, the word "Mecca" is often used as a metaphor for many shrines - Nashville is referred to as the "Mecca of Country Music", for example.

I am a Muslim and ought to go to Mecca for pilgrimage. Instead, I am drawn to the baseball shrine in Cooperstown. I mean no irreverence or sacrilege to my religion and its shrine. I hold my religion in the highest esteem and I hope to go to Mecca someday. In the meantime, I plan on making that annual pilgrimage to the National Baseball Hall of Fame. In the following pages, I will explain why Cooperstown is my Mecca.

CHAPTER I

THE CONVERSION

I was born in Guyana, (formerly British Guiana), in South America and grew up playing - and loving - cricket. No baseball was played in Guyana in those days and as far as I can ascertain, none is played today. I had, of course, heard of Babe Ruth and I read of Roy Campanella. That was the total extent of my knowledge of the game of baseball.

In 1972 I emigrated to Canada and in 1977, with the advent of the Toronto Blue Jays, I saw my first "live" ball game. By 1978 I was interested enough to take five hundred students to a ball game as part of the orientation activities of Ryerson Polytechnical Institute[1]. I was even accorded the privilege of meeting manager Roy Hartsfield on the playing field as part of the Ryerson Shinerama activities - a project in which students shine shoes to raise funds for the Cystic Fibrosis Foundation. I continued however, to regard cricket as my number one game and often played cricket matches during the summer.

My interest in baseball increased in the early 1980's and I found myself attending more and more ball games and playing less and less cricket. By 1982, I had become a Blue Jays "regular" and attended about seventy-five home games that season, a practice which continues to this day. As my interest in baseball grew so did my thirst for knowledge. I picked up as many games as I could on TV and radio. I was particularly impressed with former New York Yankees shortstop Tony Kubek who broadcast games for the Toronto Blue Jays over a local TV station. Mr. Kubek gave me new insights into the game of baseball. His commentary during games would be liberally interspersed with statistics and references to former players.

Mr. Kubek frequently mentioned the name Ty Cobb when referring to certain aspects of the game. Driven by curiosity, I bought the book <u>Ty Cobb</u> by Charles C. Alexander. It was the first of hundreds of books, magazines and other baseball publications that I would acquire. Tony Kubek opened for me the door to a whole new world. As I delved into baseball literature three truths became evident. The first was the inadequacy of my knowledge of baseball

---

1. *It is now Ryerson University.*

1

and its history. The second was the rich tradition and the wondrous store of information available to the inquiring mind in the baseball world and thirdly, there was the inveteracy of baseball in the fabric of American life.

The more I pored over my books, the more I became enamoured of players from the days of yore. I soon found myself vicariously, through my reading, a spectator, a fan, at some of baseball's most momentous games. By this time I had graduated from being merely a Blue Jays fan and had become a *baseball* fan.

My books made me feel as though I were present when James "Pud" Galvin won his twenty-first game in 1888 to become baseball's first 300-game winner. I witnessed New York Giants' Christy Mathewson pitch three shutouts in six days in the 1905 World Series against the Philadelphia Athletics. On October 2, 1908, Addie Joss of Cleveland pitched a perfect game against Ed Walsh of the Chicago White Sox. The score was 1-0. I was there to see Joss outshine Walsh who went on to win forty games that year. I saw the Cubs' "Gabby" Hartnett hit his "homer in the gloaming" against the Pirates in Wrigley Field in September 1938. More recently, I was among those fans on Coogan's Bluff overlooking the Polo Grounds on October 3, 1951 when Bobby Thomson hit "the shot heard 'round the world", to propel the Giants over the Dodgers in the final game of a three-game playoff series, thereby giving the Giants the National League Pennant.

The history of baseball became my major preoccupation. I exhausted the local public library and every other available source of reading material. As I delved deeper into baseball's past starting in early 1984, I found myself envying the generations of men and women who grew up in America and were fortunate to witness the deeds of the game's immortals like Honus Wagner, Walter Johnson, Babe Ruth, Ty Cobb, John McGraw, Ted Williams, Jackie Robinson, Mickey Mantle and Willie Mays. I sensed a void in my life, an emptiness that impelled me to make up for those lost years by learning everything I could about the game and stars of seasons past. As a consequence, I became acutely aware of the importance of the Hall of Fame as an integral part of my baseball education. I resolved to visit the Hall of Fame soon.

On two occasions, in 1981 and 1984, I attempted to visit the shrine; I had travelled to New York City to spend my vacations with my brother Wally and his family. As I drove on thruway 90 and saw the Cooperstown exit I was

2

tempted to head in that direction and spend a few hours at the Hall of Fame. I am glad I resisted the urge to do so on both occasions. A documentary on the Hall of Fame, narrated by actor Donald Sutherland, made it abundantly clear that I could not do justice to baseball's holiest shrine in a short period. Many hours of careful observation were required for one to truly absorb the grandeur of the National Baseball Hall of Fame and Museum. The time for a visit was near at hand. I set my sights on a trip in 1986.

In preparation for my visit, I set about in the winter of 1984 to learn as much as I could about the Hall of Fame and the village of Cooperstown. I even reread James Fenimore Cooper's Leatherstocking Tales, a series of five books, dealing with frontier life in the Cooperstown area. As a youngster I had read the Leatherstocking Tales; now I was soon going to visit the area once traversed by Cooper's characters, Natty Bumppo and Chingachgook. I tried to visualize the inside of the Hall of Fame; I pictured farmer Elihu Phinney's cowpasture[2] being converted into a baseball field by Abner Doubleday. I agonized over the fact that there is a solid body of evidence to disprove claims that Doubleday was responsible for starting baseball in Cooperstown. Was Cooperstown the legitimate birthplace of the National Pastime? Would I be a believer? Would I be disappointed? Would my respect and admiration for the luminaries enshrined in the Hall be reinforced or diminished by going to Cooperstown? I was certain that I had to clear up the ambivalent feelings which gripped me. I began making plans for my maiden trip to Cooperstown and the Hall of Fame for the 1986 Induction Ceremonies.

---

2. *Doubleday Field was once a cowpasture owned by Cooperstown resident Elihu Phinney. The first baseball game, supposedly organized by Abner Doubleday, was played on that cowpasture in 1839. When organized baseball accepted a report deeming Cooperstown the "birthplace of baseball", residents of the Village raised money and purchased the Phinney plot, upon which they built a baseball park and memorial to honour Doubleday. The park was officially opened in 1920.*

CHAPTER II

THE FIRST JOURNEY: AUGUST 2, 1986

Saturday morning August 2, 1986 - the beginning of my first journey. I had chosen the date carefully to coincide with the induction of new members into the Hall. High attendance and activity levels at the Hall of Fame in particular, as well as in Cooperstown in general, would mark the event. I would also be able to see some of the great men about whom I had heard and read, as it was customary for Hall of Fame members to return for the enshrinement of new members. I slept very little that Friday night, lying awake in bed thinking about my journey to Cooperstown. The thought of seeing those men filled me with excitement and the anticipation made me feel as anxious as a child on Christmas Eve awaiting the arrival of the morning. I was up and ready by 4:30 a.m.

I picked up my friend Peter Ayow and his son Barry and we set out on Highway 401 east around 5:00 a.m. Our route brought us to Gananoque, Ontario where we crossed over to the USA, on to Highway 81, then south to Thruway 90. On the way we passed Syracuse, home of the Syracuse Chiefs, the Toronto Blue Jays Triple "A" farm team. Thruway 90 east took us to the city of Utica, some 40 miles from Cooperstown and to the motel where we were staying, as accommodations in Cooperstown for the Induction Weekend are at a premium. We arrived shortly before noon, a journey of slightly less than seven hours.

In the afternoon, we travelled to Cooperstown by way of Highway 5 east and Route 28 south. On the way, we passed through several small villages and towns: Mohawk, Richfield Springs, Schuyler Lake and Fly Creek. This route travels through some of the most picturesque countryside my eyes had ever beheld: the terrain consists of rolling hills and the road appears to be a series of undulations, winding its way to our destination. Alternately, stretches of shrubs, grassland and crops, line both sides of the road. Tall trees provide shade for long stretches along the route. Here and there, a lone individual or a few people could be seen working in the yard or selling fruits and vegetables by the roadside. Houses are spaced far apart and farm houses and barns are set well away from the homes. Sheep, cattle and horses graze lazily in the mid-

Entering the Village of Fly Creek

afternoon sun. A lush, verdant countryside presents itself as far as the eye could see. Everything seems unspoiled and rustic.

As we drove along, I wondered about the suitability of the area for baseball. It seemed unlikely that so uneven a terrain would give birth to a game like baseball, requiring as it does a large, flat playing field. Why here? Why not a more suitable geography, say the flatlands of Texas or South Dakota or other parts of the Great Plains, I pondered? Yet here we were driving among the rolling hills, approaching the very spot where baseball is said to have originated.

Presently, we came to Fly Creek, a tiny village with a population of about three hundred and fifty. A wave of excitement overcame me. My heart beat faster: this was the village where *the* ball was discovered. It was here among the belongings of Abner Graves that an old, battered baseball was found in a trunk in the attic of a farmhouse, a ball that lent credence to earlier testimony given by Graves that Abner Doubleday invented baseball.[1] The ball, quite appropriately, was named the "Doubleday Baseball" and was among the first artifacts to be exhibited in Cooperstown.

I knew Cooperstown was close. Minutes later we came upon the following sign:

BICENTENNIAL VILLAGE
1786-1986
WELCOME TO
COOPERSTOWN,N.Y.,
on OTSEGO LAKE
ELEVATION 1264 FT.
HOME OF BASEBALL
VILLAGE OF MUSEUMS

We had arrived. One final, long bend in the road and we were in Cooperstown. We had left Utica just after one o'clock and reached Cooperstown less than an hour later.

---

1.   *Abner Graves claimed to have been present when the game organized by Doubleday was played in Cooperstown in 1839.*

Sign on the outskirts of Cooperstown approaching from Route 28 South.

The village of Cooperstown, boasting a population of slightly over three thousand, two hundred inhabitants, is situated in the central part of the state of New York, about seventy miles west of the state capital, Albany and thirty miles south of New York State Thruway 90. Cooperstown is named after Judge William Cooper, father of the author James Fenimore Cooper. The elder Cooper, while living with his family in Burlington, New Jersey acquired land in the Lake Otsego area. In 1785, Judge Cooper visited the area, then uninhabited, for the first time. To encourage settlement, he sold 40,000 acres of land cheaply to immigrants and moved to Cooperstown permanently with his family in 1786.

Located away from established routes and thoroughfares, the Village has been able to preserve much of its idyllic beauty: a canal, a railroad and two interstate highways have all bypassed Cooperstown. James Fenimore Cooper with a remarkable degree of prescience stated in 1838:

> We shall have no mushroom city, but there is little doubt that ... as the population of the country fills up, this spot will contain a provincial town of importance. The beauty of its situation, the lake, the purity of the air, and the other advantages ... seem destined to make it all peculiarly a place of resort ... for the inhabitants of the large towns during the warm months. (A View from Mt.Vision; A Brief History of Cooperstown, (as quoted in the Cooperstown Area Guide), 1986, (p.6)

Another notable family, the Clarks, later played a major role in furthering the quality of life in the community. Their affiliation with the Singer Sewing Machine Company made the Clark family very wealthy. Through their philanthropy, numerous facilities and services were established, including the Baseball Hall of Fame, the New York State Historical Association, The Farmers' Museum, Fenimore House, a hospital, a scholarship fund and a gymnasium.

The Coopers, chiefly through James Fenimore, were responsible for bringing Cooperstown to the rest of America and the world; the Clarks, through their generosity and civic pride, opened up Cooperstown to the rest of America and the world. In the process, Cooper's 1838 prediction was realized. His books allow readers to learn about Cooperstown and whet their appetite for the region; the Clarks donated the facilities that now service thousands of visitors who come in response.

Route 28 leads to Chestnut Street. A sign indicates that a left turn (north on Chestnut), would take us in the direction of the Hall of Fame. We had gone scarcely one hundred yards when I noticed the Chamber of Commerce building to our right. We parked across the street and went to the office, a small two-storeyed building. On the first floor, about the size of an average living room, were two persons behind a counter, answering inquiries ranging from directions to the Hall of Fame to finding accommodation for visitors. A multiplicity of pamphlets, booklets, postcards and magazines were neatly stacked on racks and desks. Of particular interest was a brochure entitled, Cooperstown Bicentennial, listing events for the Bicentennial year (1986), from January to December. There was also a two page, legal sized sheet called Happenings, which detailed events from Friday, August 1, to Thursday, August 7. We took copies of these and other relevant publications and walked over to Doubleday Field. My intention at the time was to do a quick survey of the Village to identify key points and places of interest, with a view to making more leisurely visits later during the weekend. Doubleday Field is located behind the Chamber of Commerce building, between Chestnut Street on the west and Main street on the north. It has an intimate appearance: short-cropped, dark green grass and yellowish-brown dirt that covers the pitcher's mound, batter's box and baselines. Behind home plate is a small covered section of seats reserved for dignitaries. Directly below is the dugout, tiny by major league proportions. Open stands run along the left side to the point where left field begins, while on the right, more open stands run from about first base to roughly left-centre field. The outfield is bordered by a fence that separates the park from the backyards of homes. I said to myself, "So this is where it all started!"

Facing Main Street to the north of Doubleday Field is Doubleday Plaza parking lot which is fringed with shops to the left and right. We wandered to the left, stopping at *Baseball Nostalgia*, a store with a wide assortment of baseball-related items. Doubleday Batting Range is housed in the same building and we watched people paying to take swings in the cage, while in another corner, newspaper headlines were being made to order for only five dollars. Walking north through the parking lot, I noticed on the northeast corner, just inside the entrance from Main Street, a bronzed statue now turned green by

The Cooperstown Chamber of Commerce Office Building

11

the night air. The form was unmistakeable: a ballplayer, bat on shoulder, ready for the pitch. This was "The Sand Lot Kid", a statue that was erected as a tribute to all the youngsters who play baseball on the sandlots of America.

Turning east on Main Street, we headed for the Hall. Main Street was a hive of activity: sidewalks crowded with people wearing shirts and caps representing many of the Major League teams and stores laden with baseball merchandise, doing brisk business. The license plates of the cars parked on both sides of the street told their own story: devotees from faraway California to nearby New Jersey were here to worship.

At last we came to the Hall of Fame. I had arrived at the Shrine. One final act remained for me to complete my pilgrimage: I had to go through the Hall. I would do that tomorrow but for now I was content to gaze upon the building and watch the steady throng entering and exiting the Hall.

The structure that houses the Hall of Fame has three levels with a triangular-shaped roof of grey slate. Rows of windows fringe the building and the entire facility is constructed of brown coloured, fireproof brick and stone. The building is divided into three interconnected sections. Two corner sections rise from the sidewalk. The middle part, about forty feet wide, rises some twenty feet inward from the edge of the sidewalk forming a little courtyard. Facing the building on the left side of the courtyard, hoisted on a flagpole, is Old Glory, while the Hall of Fame ensign flies on a pole on the right side. A few benches provide a place of rest for weary travellers. Four steps, carved out of white marble with wrought iron hand rails painted black, lead to a large arch-shaped portal. Two smaller openings, also arch-shaped, frame the main doorway and provide access for visitors to the Hall of Fame.

The National Baseball Library sits behind the Hall of Fame. Established in 1939 for the purpose of collecting and preserving documents related to baseball, the Library was originally housed in the same building as the Hall of Fame and the Museum but gradually outgrew its first quarters and moved to its present building in 1968. Information on every topic pertaining to baseball can be found in the over 150,000 photographs, multitude of publications and exhaustive biographical information on players, umpires, broadcasters and sportswriters that comprise the Library's collection. Like the Museum, the Library relies on the goodwill of fans, collectors and players to acquire items. A professional librarian and research staff are available to assist with requests,

THE ENTRANCE TO COOPER PARK

and services are also available by telephone or through the mail.[2] With the exception of national holidays and the limited access on Saturdays and Sundays from June to September, the library is open to the public year round.

Facing the Library is Cooper Park; it is spacious with an ample supply of shrubs and tall trees that give shade to the bright green lawns spread through-out the park. Immediately in front of the Library is a large open space, guard-ed by a statue of James Fenimore Cooper. It is in this area that people formerly gathered to witness the Induction Ceremonies. We returned to Main Street, walked east a short distance to Fair Street then north on Fair Street to Lakefront Park.

As we approached I beheld the Otsego in all its majesty. This was "Lake Glimmerglass" as Cooper had described it in *The Deerslayer*:

> ... a broad sheet of water, so placid and limpid
> that it resembled a bed of pure mountain atmosphere
> compressed into a setting of hills and woods....Its
> margin was irregular, being indented by bays and broken
> by many projecting low points. ... the most striking
>   peculiarities of the scene were its solemn solitude and
> sweet repose. On all sides, wherever the eye turned,
>   nothing met it but the mirrorlike surface of the lake,
> the placid view of heaven. (p.27 and p.28)

The lake, some one hundred and sixty feet at its deepest point, is nine miles long and approximately half a mile wide, except along Glimmerglass Park where it widens to about a mile. Thickly forested hills rise from the banks of the lake. Sailboats and yachts deck the surface and anglers seeking the bass, trout, salmon and pickerel that abound in the lake cast their lines from station-ary boats or from points where the land juts out into the water. At the nearby pier, departure point for the Lake Otsego boat tours, I looked into water so clear that I could see the bottom of the lake. Its depth ranges from about ten feet at the water's edge to more than twenty feet farther out on the pier. Ducks paddled along, occasionally diving below to catch some of the smaller fish frolicking among the larger specimen. All of this was clearly visible for several feet from the shore.

2.   *See Appendix B for a detailed description of the Library and its services.*

The Mouth of the Susquehanna River

Boat tours take place on the *Narra Mattah and the Chief Uncas*. The *Chief Uncas* is a yacht built in 1912 for the Busch family of St. Louis Cardinals and Budweiser Beer fame. Typical of the boats of the era, the *Chief Uncas* is built of mahogany and features fine leather seats. The Busch family, longtime property owners on the lake, allow the boat to be used for tours. A guide provides a running commentary on the various points of interest, among them Kingfisher Tower, Sunken Islands and Fenimore House. The Otsego is usually a hub of activity: scores of boats sail in every direction, waterskiers plane its surface and swimmers frolic in its clear water. All this is a far cry from the tranquil days when Hawkeye and Chingachgook paddled on Lake Glimmerglass, and yet one hundred and fifty years later, the Otsego still maintains much of its pristine beauty.

With my back to the lake, I scanned the surrounding tree line for other landmarks described by Cooper. Slightly to my left, about two hundred yards ahead and rising a few feet above the water, sits Council Rock, an Indians meeting place. Otsego is an Indian word for *place of the meeting*, and the lake derives its name from the Indians meeting at the rock. A few yards away from Council Rock, partially hidden by thick foliage, the Otsego narrows to form the beginning of the Susquehanna River which wends its way for 444 miles through New York, Pennsylvania and Maryland. I savoured this panorama and marvelled at the realization of what I was seeing. When I read the Leatherstocking Tales as a young boy, so long ago and so far away, little did I think that someday I would be able to gaze upon Lake Glimmerglass, Council Rock and the Susquehanna as Hawkeye and Chingachgook had done in Fenimore Cooper's tales.

All this preoccupation with the history and beauty of the land did not make me lose sight of the people around me. Visitors, distinguished by their base-ball regalia, and the village folk alike crowded the streets, the stores and the sidewalks. The village folk were cheerfully giving directions or serving cus-tomers in stores, while others sat in the parks or on wrought iron benches on the sidewalk. The Atlanta Journal, in an article in the 1986 Cooperstown Area Guide, describes Cooperstown as follows:

> The air is so fresh and cool and rejuvenating. The sun
> is so bright, glistening so splendidly off Lake Otsego.
> The people are so friendly, the pace so relaxed. ... it

is a tourist attraction...a community that functions on
one traffic light despite the annual influx of more than
200,000 guests. If this were not a shrine to baseball,
it would be a shrine to small town, USA. (p.14)

I bought souvenirs from stores on Main Street and from vendors on the sidewalk. We walked west along Main Street to Chestnut Street, the intersection featuring the only traffic lights in Cooperstown. Proceeding north on Chestnut, we turned left on Lake Street. One hundred and fifty yards away on the north side of Lake Street stood the Otesaga Hotel, a massive structure of stone resembling an old English castle. It is here that the Hall of Fame members stay when they come for the Induction Ceremonies. Facing the hotel to my right was a temporary ten-foot wide passage fenced on both sides by four-foot high pickets, held together by wire. This passage led from the sidewalk to the back of the hotel and was used to provide access to an autograph session held earlier in the day by the Members of the Hall of Fame.

As dusk set in we returned to our car and headed back to Utica and settled in our motel rooms for the night. I reflected on how eventful my day had been and fell asleep with visions of what new wonders and excitement lay in store for me the following day.

CHAPTER III

GODS AMONG MEN

Early in the morning of Sunday August 3, we left Utica for Cooperstown. Arriving around 7:00 a.m., we parked across the street from the Chamber of Commerce office. The stillness of the Village that morning reminded me of a remark made by Honus Wagner, the "Flying Dutchman", on his induction in 1939: " A nice, quiet town you have here. It reminds me of Sleepy Hollow" (as quoted in Baseball's Hall of Fame, 1981, p.14).

The Village slowly came alive with activity. Cars with mostly out of state licence plates, drove up and down the streets, trying to find parking. Sidewalk vendors were busily emptying cartons and arranging the contents on display tables to attract customers: T-shirts, autographed bats, baseballs and photographs, envelopes with portraits of the inductees, ceramic mugs, glassware and books. The smell of muffins, hot dogs and coffee wafted through the cool, morning air. We had breakfast at the Short Stop restaurant, where the servings were plentiful and cost very little. The Hall of Fame beckoned so we headed off in that direction. We had a twenty-minute wait to the 9:00 a.m. opening time. Like John Keats' "Naughty Boy" who stood in his shoes and wondered, I stood among the crowd and wondered what it would be like going through the Hall.

The National Baseball Hall of Fame and Museum was officially opened on June 12, 1939. Originally, some Cooperstown civic leaders and baseball dignitaries had intended to establish a National Baseball Museum but that plan was expanded to include a Hall of Fame. Earlier in the century it had been determined, though under somewhat questionable circumstances, that Cooperstown was the home of baseball. A Commission, comprised of seven prominent Americans, was appointed in 1905 to look into the origins of baseball. Commission members included a former State Governor, a US Senator, baseball league executives and former baseball players. After receiving testimony for three years, the Commission, in a burst of patriotism, declared that "the first scheme for playing baseball according to the best evidence obtainable to date, was devised by Abner Doubleday at Cooperstown, N.Y., in 1839" (National Baseball Hall of Fame and Museum Yearbook, 1987, p.7).

The Babe greets visitors inside the Hall of Fame

This conclusion was based chiefly upon the evidence of Abner Graves (mentioned earlier), who claimed that he was present in 1839 when Abner Doubleday organized the first baseball game. Most serious students and historians of the game discount the Doubleday theory. Documents have since shown that Doubleday was a cadet at the West Point Military Academy in 1839 and could not therefore, have been in Cooperstown as alleged. Besides, although Doubleday kept careful records, there is no mention of baseball in Cooperstown, in any of his diaries. An abundance of evidence exists to show that baseball has its origin in the English game of rounders.

Organized baseball, nonetheless, accepted the Commission's findings and deemed Cooperstown the birthplace of baseball. When discussions got underway in 1935 to find a suitable museum for a number of baseball artifacts that had been acquired, Ford Frick, then President of the National League, proposed the founding of a Hall of Fame as well, to honour baseball's greatest heroes.

Frick's suggestion was enthusiastically received and dove-tailed perfectly with plans that were being formulated to celebrate the Centennial of baseball in 1939. The Baseball Writers' Association of America was asked to choose the members to be enshrined in the Hall of Fame. In 1936, the writers chose five players as the first tenants of the Hall: Ty Cobb, Babe Ruth, Honus Wagner, Christy Mathewson and Walter Johnson. Unquestionably, no other single group represents, or is likely to represent, greater achievement in baseball than these five immortals. In the ensuing years leading to the first Induction Ceremonies in 1939, twenty-one more of baseball's finest were selected for entry into the Hall.

A distant church bell chiming nine o'clock brought me back from my musing. Now it was *my* time to enter the Hall. A five-dollar entrance fee got me a ticket and I passed through a turnstile after receiving a stamp on the back of my hand, a stamp that allows visitors to exit and re-enter the Hall on the same day without further payment. Upon entering the Hall, Babe Ruth stood directly before me, bat over his shoulder, ready to swing and so incredibly life-like that I was startled. It took me several seconds to realize that this was a life-sized wood carving. Nearby, also prominently positioned, was an equally impressive carving of the Red Sox's No.9, the Kid, the Splendid Splinter, Ted

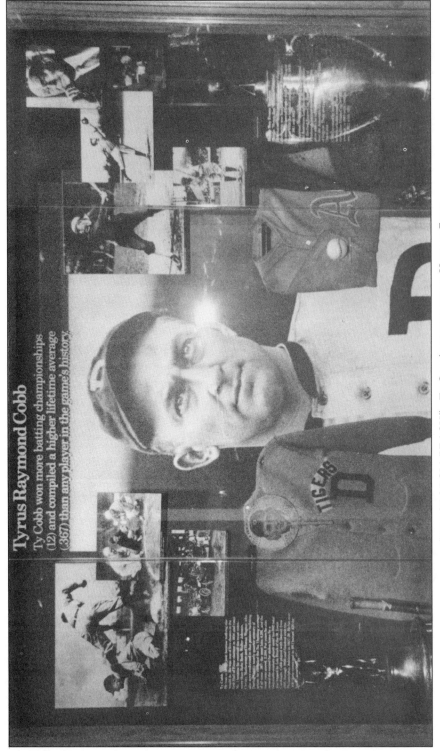

Tyrus Raymond Cobb

Ty Cobb won more batting championships (12) and compiled a higher lifetime average (367) than any player in the game's history.

"THE GEORGIA PEACH" - TY COBB'S EXHIBIT IN THE HALL OF FAME

Williams. I picked up a brochure entitled "Guide to Exhibits", and set out on my journey through the Hall.

On the first floor were housed the Cooperstown Room, the Great Moments Room and the Hall of Fame Gallery. I looked at the features of the other levels and decided to leave the first floor for last, as the exhibits on that floor seemed to me to be of greater significance and would require more attention. As I walked up the stairs to the second floor, I faced large silk-screen portraits of the three persons who would be inducted into the Hall later that day: Willie McCovey, Bobby Doerr and Ernie Lombardi.

Upon reaching the second floor, the first display that caught my eye was that of Ty Cobb. A large portrait of the "Georgia Peach" towered above the many items that belonged to him: a sweatshirt, baseball shoes, trophies, photographs. I had come a long way from the time I first heard Tony Kubek mention the name Ty Cobb. Standing there, looking at his picture, I felt a little sad and cheated: I wanted to have seen him play. To my right stood a display case with Cy Young's memorabilia - a photograph of his car, licence plate reading C511Y (511 lifetime victories), trophies and items of his uniform.

Moving slowly from section to section, I absorbed as much as possible about General History, Black Baseball, Evolution of Equipment, Casey Stengel, World Tours and All-Star games. From time to time I lingered as I recognized an artifact about which I had read, or to pick up new bits and pieces of information. The "Old Perfesser", Casey Stengel, had the largest collection of items on display: numerous photographs, trophies, awards, uniforms, bats, all overshadowed by a blown-up photograph of Casey making a point.

Moving up to the third floor, I spent a considerable time at the Babe Ruth display which depicts his locker surrounded by the bat and ball of his 60th home run (hit in 1927), his New York Yankees uniform, trophies and photographs highlighting his career. The Ball Parks Section gave me a glimpse of some of the old stadia which had passed on into history - Crosley Field (Cincinnati), Ebbets Field (New York City), Forbes Field (Pittsburgh), the Polo Grounds (New York City) and Shibe Park (Philadelphia). An impressive array of baseball cards also attracted my attention, among them the most expensive card of all, the T-206 Honus Wagner tobacco card. The World Series room reflected heroes and special moments of the Fall Classic, a display comple-

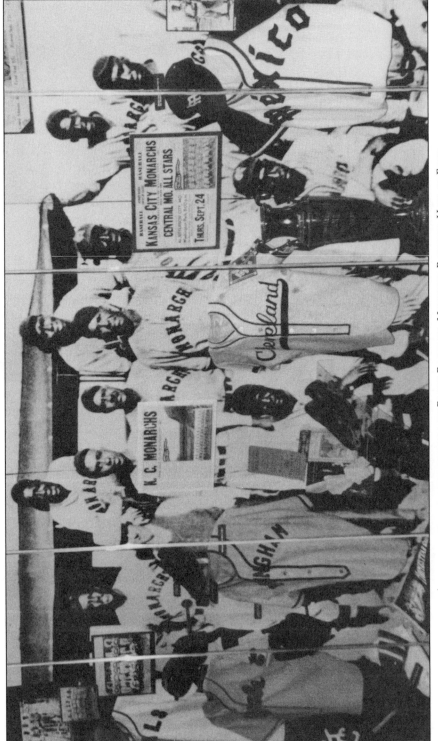

24

mented by World Series programmes and rings. Exhibits of Minor League and Youth Baseball completed the floor.

I then returned to the first floor to the Great Moments Room where large blown-ups brought to life some of the unforgettable moments of the sport: the Babe's 60th home run in 1927; Lou Gehrig's 2,130 consecutive games streak - June 1, 1925 to April 30, 1939; Joe DiMaggio's fifty-six-game hitting streak in 1941; the Splendid Splinter's .406 batting average in 1941; Jackie Robinson's debut with the Brooklyn Dodgers - the first black to play in the Major Leagues in the modern era; Bobby Thomson's "shot heard 'round the world", October 3, 1951. Overhead television monitors carried Mel Allen's "This Week in Baseball".

I next visited the Cooperstown Room in which a myriad of displays, photographs and paintings traced the origin of baseball and the progress of the Museum through the years. There, in a glass case, all by itself, sat the Abner Doubleday Baseball, found among Abner Graves' belongings in 1935. Also featured were mementoes of previous years' Induction Ceremonies. Most striking of all was a blow up which covered a whole wall, a photograph of ten of the Hall of Fame members who had attended the first Induction Ceremonies in 1939: Eddie Collins, Babe Ruth, Connie Mack, Cy Young, Honus Wagner, Grover Cleveland Alexander, Tris Speaker, Nap Lajoie, George Sisler and Walter Johnson.[1]

Finally, the *pièce de résistance*: the Hall of Fame Gallery. Immediately upon entering I felt as though I stepped into a church. A short passage down a relatively dark and somewhat narrow corridor leads visitors into the Gallery, a room which even on the darkest of days or when full of visitors, seems spacious and filled with light. Blond wood panels seem to soar to the high ceiling forming the series of small alcoves that fringe the Gallery, each alcove gleaming quietly with the burnished bronze plaques of the Inductees, each plaque detailing highlights of that particular immortal's career. In the centre of this seemingly vast space stands a majestic wooden column on which are mounted the plaques of the Inductees for the current year. Underfoot, a thick carpet in a majestic deep red muffles the footsteps of the visitors as they move from alcove to alcove. A respectful silence pervades the gallery and people speak in

---

1.   *Ty Cobb, also an inaugural year inductee, unfortunately arrived after the picture had been taken.*

IN THE COOPERSTOWN ROOM SITTING IN FRONT OF A BLOWN UP PHOTOGRAPH FEATURING TEN OF THE ELEVEN HALL OF FAMERS WHO ATTENDED THE FIRST INDUCTION CEREMONIES ON JUNE 12, 1939. STANDING: HONUS WAGNER, GROVER CLEVELAND ALEXANDER, TRIS SPEAKER, NAP LAJOIE, GEORGE SISLER AND WALTER JOHNSON. SEATED: EDDIE COLLINS, BABE RUTH, CONNIE MACK AND CY YOUNG.

whispers as though reluctant to disturb the heroes who repose in that hallowed chamber.

I read some of the plaques and their inscriptions as I moved among the crowd that had, by this time, come into this section of the Hall. On the plaque of the "Big Train", Walter Johnson, the workhorse of the Washington Senators from 1907 to 1927, I noticed the 414 victories recorded at the time of his induction. It was later discovered that he did, in fact, win 416 games but the plaque was not modified to reflect this fact. It did not matter to me - and I suspect, to countless millions of other fans - for two fewer victories could not detract from Johnson's incredible record which was achieved despite pitching for the Senators, a consistently weak team. His victories are second only to Cy Young's 511 and Johnson's 110 shutouts are a record. When he retired in 1927, he held the strikeout record with 3,508; that has since been eclipsed by only six pitchers.[2] Several yards down the hall, I looked at Joe Sewell who played shortstop for the Cleveland Indians and New York Yankees. Sewell was remarkable for his phenomenal, low strikeout record: he struck out only 114 times in fourteen seasons and played five seasons in which he had 4 or fewer strikeouts. Once, in over 437 at-bats and 115 games, he did not strike out at all.

Legitimacy, disappointment, ambivalence were but some of the words that had come to mind as I prepared for my visit to Cooperstown. Now, they had all vanished. The merits or lack thereof, of the Doubleday proposition no longer mattered. What mattered was that Cooperstown was the Shrine of Baseball and a more desirable home for baseball's immortals would be difficult to find. When I finally ended my tour of the Hall of Fame, I concluded that I had surely come to a sacred place. I sincerely believed that the spiritual upliftment I experienced as I gazed upon those plaques in the baseball Shrine in Cooperstown, New York, was no less uplifting than that which I would feel at the Shrine of my religion in Arabia. Within the walls of the Hall of Fame resided heroes who were truly gods among men, immortalized in the hearts and minds of tens of millions of baseball fans like myself. Cooperstown was indeed, my Mecca.

---

2.   *The six pitchers who have exceeded this record are Bert Blyleven, Steve Carlton, Gaylord Perry, Nolan Ryan, Tom Seaver, and Don Sutton.*

CHAPTER IV

"THEY STARTED SOMETHING HERE" - Babe Ruth

After my visit to the Hall, my friends and I went to Cooper Park. Several hundred people had gathered to await the start of the Induction Ceremonies. With a little over an hour to spare, I decided to take a boat tour of Lake Otsego, so I set out for Lakefront Park, purchased a ticket and boarded the *Chief Uncas* for the hour-long tour.

Returning to Cooper Park from Lakefront Park, I was not prepared for the spectacle that awaited me. In the hour since I had left for the boat tour, the crowd of several hundred had swelled to about nine or ten thousand persons assembled throughout the park. A large part of the lawn in front of the Baseball Library was blocked off by a four-foot high green, temporary picket fence, and several rows of chairs were neatly arranged on the lawn. This was the area reserved for dignitaries, spouses and relatives and friends of Hall of Famers, other special invitees and the media. Most of the chairs were occupied and a steady stream of guests quickly filled the remaining seats. Radio and TV crews, photographers and writers, were busily preparing for the impending Ceremonies; red, white and blue buntings were draped along the fence and on the temporary platform that had been erected as an extension to the front of the Baseball Library.

I wended my way through a maze of people and lawn chairs, to a spot I had chosen earlier. Much to my chagrin, I soon realized that the space was already occupied. Dejected, I tried to find another place from which to watch the proceedings. While trying to find another spot I met Lou Gillick, an acquaintance from Toronto who offered to share his space with me. I gladly accepted and settled down to await the Induction Ceremonies. As I chatted with Lou Gillick and other fans nearby, I found that many of them were returnees: "regulars" who attended the Induction Ceremonies every year. I learned also that Induction Day envelopes were on sale by vendors on the Main Street sidewalk.

My viewing position secure, I went in search of the Induction Day Covers. I located a vendor and bought two identical envelopes for four dollars each.

The Otsego in Late Summer

Hand-drawn portraits of Ernie Lombardi, Willie McCovey and Bobby Doerr adorned the left hand side of the cover with the words "Induction Day, August 3, 1986" printed above and "Cooperstown, N.Y." below. I took the envelopes to the post office, across the street from the Hall of Fame, affixed twenty-two cents postage stamps on each and had them cancelled. The postmark consisted of a circle with "Cooperstown, N.Y.,13326, August 3, 1986" printed inside the circle; four horizontal bars with "Induction Day Sta" printed on one of the bars, completed the postmark. As a public service to the Hall of Fame and to baseball fans, the Cooperstown post office is opened on Induction Day (Sunday), to facilitate philatelists and souvenir collectors in obtaining Induction Day Covers.

On my way back to Cooper Park it started to rain - a light, gentle rain. It was as if Providence was intervening to shower its blessings upon the function that was just about to commence. I collected a programme - the Forty-Seventh Annual Programme - courtesy of the Sporting News, and rejoined the Gillicks. Presently, Tracy Ringolsby of the Dallas Morning News and President of the Baseball Writers' Association of America, took the microphone in his capacity as Master of Ceremonies. The proceedings were underway.

After brief remarks by Mr. Ringolsby, George Grande of ESPN took over. He introduced the Hall of Famers, touching briefly on the highlights of each immortal's career. One by one they came - Warren Spahn, Judy Johnson, Bob Lemon, Hank Aaron, Charlie Gehringer, Ernie Banks, "Jocko" Conlan, Stan Musial, Ted Williams, Ralph Kiner, Joe Sewell, Monte Irvin, Billy Herman, "Lefty" Gomez, Johnny Mize, Roy Campanella, Al Lopez,"Pee Wee" Reese, Robin Roberts, "Cool Papa" Bell, "Happy" Chandler and Enos Slaughter. All together twenty-four Hall of Famers were present, including Willie McCovey and Bobby Doerr.

Following prayers by Reverend Canon Blomquist, a moment of silence was observed in tribute to the baseball people who had passed away since the last Induction Ceremonies. Steven Owen of the local Glimmerglass Opera gave a stirring rendition of the National Anthem and Cooperstown Mayor Harold Hollis, formally welcomed everyone to Cooperstown and to the Induction Ceremonies. Awards were then presented to media members.

Earl Lawson was presented with the J.G. Taylor Spink Award for 1985. Established in 1962 in honour of J. G. Taylor Spink, the late owner/publisher

Chief Uncas - ready for the next tour

of The Sporting News, the award is given to sports writers "for meritorious contributions to baseball writing". The winner is honoured in the year following selection. Lawson began as a copy boy for the Cincinnati Times-Star. When the paper folded in 1958, Lawson moved to the Cincinnati Post where he stayed until his retirement in 1985. He covered the Big Red Machine of the 1970's and held the office of President of the Baseball Writers' Association of America in 1977.

Bob Prince whose career spanned five decades, was honoured posthumously with the Ford C. Frick Award "for major contributions to the game of baseball". This award was established for broadcasters in 1978, in memory of Ford Frick who was one of the earliest broadcasters before becoming President of the National League then Baseball Commissioner.

Prince's broadcasting career started in 1941 and reached prominence when he joined the Pittsburgh Pirates broadcasting team (radio station KDKA) in the late 1940's. Prince's unabashed partisanship of the Pirates was reflected in his broadcasts. He was as well known for his colourful baseball language as he was for his fancy sports jackets. Bob Prince also covered hockey, football and boxing, and was play-by-play man for ABC's Monday Night Baseball telecasts for a while.

Several distinguished guests were then introduced, guests who were seated among the crowd on the lawn and who included baseball executives and relatives of the Hall of Famers. Ed Stack, President of the Hall of Fame, was next introduced followed by the Commissioner of Baseball, Peter Ueberroth who conducted the Dedication Ceremonies. On this day, we had come to witness the canonization of three of baseball's immortals - Ernie Lombardi, Bobby Doerr and Willie McCovey.

Commissioner Ueberroth first inducted Ernie Lombardi, outlining his playing career with emphasis on significant achievements such as his MVP award in 1938. Slow of foot and nicknamed the "SCHNOZZ", Lombardi compensated for his lack of speed by his hitting, topping the .300 mark ten times and ending his seventeen-year major league tour of duty (1931-1947), with a .306 average and two batting titles. Lombardi was a catcher and played for four Major League teams - the Brooklyn Dodgers, the Cincinnati Reds, the Boston Braves and the New York Giants. The plaque was received on Lombardi's behalf by his sister Mrs. William Lenhardt. Lombardi died in 1977 and was elected to baseball's Pantheon by the Baseball Hall of Fame Committee on Baseball Veterans.

Bobby Doerr, the next inductee, was also elected by the Veterans' Committee. Doerr spent all of his major league playing days with the Boston Red Sox - fourteen seasons from 1937 to 1951 and served in the military in 1945. Mr. Doerr's accomplishments include driving in 100 or more runs on six occasions, leading American League second basemen in double plays four times and setting what was then an American League record of 414 fielding chances without an error. His team-mate Ted Williams, called him "the silent captain of the Red Sox". Bobby Doerr is a quiet, soft-spoken man. His acceptance speech was simple, short and reflective of his humble nature. As he ended, I thought of another humble player, the gentle giant Walter Johnson, inducted into the Hall of Fame some forty-seven years earlier in June 1939. With what Ken Smith describes as, "a deep and matchless humility which only the truly great know," Johnson accepted his plaque and replied, "I am glad I was able to do enough to merit an honour of this magnitude." <u>Baseball's Hall of Fame</u>, (New York: Tempo Books, Grosset and Dunlap), 1981. (p.14).

Finally, the Commissioner dedicated Willie McCovey's plaque. Elected by members of the Baseball Writers' Association of America in his first year of eligibility for enshrinement, McCovey played for twenty-two seasons in the National League, except for a very brief eleven game stint in the American League in 1976. He started and ended his major league career with the San Francisco Giants, spending a total of nineteen years with the team. "Stretch" McCovey's achievements include 521 home runs, 18 grand slams (second to Lou Gehrig's twenty-three), National League Rookie of the Year (1959), National League MVP (1969), National League Comeback Player of the Year, (1977), and league leader in home runs three times.

McCovey's acceptance speech was quite moving, focusing on his adoptive baseball family, the people who helped him throughout his playing career. The Stonehams, part of his adoptive family and owners of the Giants, were singled out for special gratitude. At one point Willie, overcome by emotion, paused for a few moments to regain his composure and there were few dry eyes among the crowd assembled in Cooper Park. McCovey ended his speech to a thunderous ovation, led by several supporters who wore orange coloured shirts with the words "McCovey's Minions" in black.

Mr. Ringolsby thanked the participants and brought the Ceremonies to a close. As we picked up our belongings and started to disperse, I reflected on the Ceremonies just concluded and how difficult it was to gain entry into the Hall of Fame. The baseball writers who had the option of electing up to ten persons, had found only Willie McCovey deserving of enshrinement. A minimum of seventy-five percent of the ballots cast is required for election. Lombardi and Doerr waited a combined seventy-three years before gaining admission, having been bypassed by the Baseball Writers' Association of America.

Early Monday morning, we returned to Cooperstown and tried to obtain tickets to the Hall of Fame game. Doubleday Field seats approximately ten thousand persons and the demand for tickets far exceeds the supply. We had hoped to buy tickets from scalpers, those unofficial ticket sellers who hang around ball parks but the prices were too steep even for enthusiastic first-time visitors like ourselves. Disappointed, we left for home.

My failure to get to see the game did not, however, detract from the euphoria I felt during the weekend and for many days afterwards. My maiden visit to the Hall of Fame was a resounding success. As we drove out of the Village on Route 28, the words spoken by Babe Ruth on the day of his Induction rang in my ears: "They started something here". (Baseball's Hall of Fame,(New York:Tempo Books, Grosset and Dunlap), 1981. (p. 17). They certainly did! I resolved to return. My love affair with the National Baseball Hall of Fame and Museum, and with Cooperstown, had begun.

CHAPTER V:

THE SECOND COMING - THE 1987 INDUCTION CEREMONIES

My appetite had been whetted by my visit to Cooperstown. I had to learn more about the operations of the Hall of Fame and Museum. In November, I mailed twenty dollars (U.S.) to the Hall of Fame for membership in the Hall of Fame Fan Club, "Friends of the Hall of Fame". In return, I received a membership card/pass which entitled me to unlimited free admission to the Hall of Fame for a year, the Hall of Fame yearbook, an embroidered patch depicting the Hall of Fame logo, an Hall of Fame T-shirt and four quarterly newsletters. I also sent for souvenirs from the Hall of Fame gift shop, including post cards of all 196 of the Hall of Fame inductees to 1986.

Although Thursday, December 18, 1986 started like any ordinary day, it was an especially momentous day for me and a far from ordinary day in the baseball world. It was the 100th Anniversary of the birth of Ty Cobb. I had looked forward to this day for more than a year, not unlike a zealot awaiting the arrival of his hero.

Over a year before, I had begun an extensive quest to have Cobb's Centennial observed. I started by writing to the Postmaster General of the United States, the Hon. William F. Bolger, asking that consideration be given to the issuance of a commemorative postage stamp. The Philatelic Communications Specialist of the Stamp Development Branch informed me that the stamp programme for 1986 had been determined prior to the receipt of my letter. I also sent this letter to President Reagan and the Editor of the Washington Post to try and enlist their support but, not unexpectedly, received no replies from them. Reasoning that some form of celebration was fitting for the man many acknowledge as the greatest Tiger ever, I wrote to the President of the Detroit Tigers Baseball Club, Tom Monaghan and sent a copy of this letter to the Detroit Free Press. Again, I received no reply. Finally, I tried to arouse officials in Cobb's native state of Georgia to take action. I wrote to the Hon. Joe Frank Harris, Governor of the State of Georgia, to the Editor of the Atlanta Constitution, to Mayor John Baird of Royston, Georgia, (where Cobb settled) and to the the Editor of the Royston News Leader. Sadly, the only apparent fruits of my labours were a copy of the <u>News Leader</u> with my letter in it and a letter from Governor Harris, in which he remarked that he was "... quite sure that the Centennial will be properly marked by the appropriate parties, and ... will look for the opportunity to offer ... support for such an effort." I was unable to determine whether or not any action was taken to honour Ty's memory.

Having failed, or at least assuming failure with officialdom, I resigned myself to awaiting December 18, 1986, to observe the Centennial in some more personal fashion. On this day I telephoned my favourite local radio station and was rewarded with an announcement on the occasion. At noon I stopped working and observed a minute's silence in memory of "The Georgia Peach". I believe he would have approved.

The off-season wore on, brightened in January by the announcement that Billy Williams and Jim "Catfish" Hunter, the only nominees able to muster the required 75% of the ballots cast by members of the Baseball Writers' Association of America, had been elected to the Hall of Fame and brightened again in March when Ray Dandridge was chosen to enter the Hall by the Committee on Baseball Veterans. By January my own off-season was assuming a pattern as I continued my development as a baseball fan. I read about baseball every day and continued to acquire baseball publications. I had also started to plan my activities for the upcoming baseball season, taking steps to secure tickets for the 1987 Hall of Fame game and mailing postcards to the Hall of Fame lottery for tickets. I also asked a few friends to enter their names, in order to enhance my chances. Although I had no luck, one of my fellow voyagers from my first visit to Cooperstown was sucessful, receiving four tickets.

In early May, I was privileged to meet Hall of Famer Enos "Country" Slaughter. He had come to Canada to participate in opening ceremonies for the Toronto Maple Leaf Baseball Club of the Inter-County Major Baseball League. At the Maple Leaf home opener, I joined other fans as Slaughter shared some of his experiences as a ball player. Asked to comment on the seeming indifference by some present day players toward fans, he remarked that athletes who let their superstar or celebrity status get to their heads, quickly come back down to earth when their playing days are over and they no longer experience the thunderous ovation and adulation of the fans.

Slaughter noted that he had become the toast of St. Louis, following his mad dash from first base to home, the dash that gave the Cardinals the victory in the 1946 World Series; he noted that his interaction with the fans lessened soon thereafter. Being in the spotlight made him tend to ignore the fans for a while and full realization of how much the fans meant to him came only when his playing days were over. A man who relishes his position among baseball's elite, Slaughter stated that as long as there was life in his body, he would attend the Hall of Fame Induction Ceremonies.

During May and June, I continued to work on arrangements for the Induction weekend - accommodation, projected expenses and an itinerary - for myself and a growing entourage of fans. Meanwhile, down at Exhibition Stadium, then home of the Toronto Blue Jays, I mounted a campaign to get Blue Jays outfielder George Bell on the All-Star team. For over a week, I carried a placard to the ballpark, exhorting fans to vote for George. Bell made the team and thus became the first Blue Jays position player in the starting line-up of the All-Star game. Bell went on to become the 1987 American League's Most Valuable Player and the Sporting News' Player of the Year.

Before I realized it, the time was near for my second pilgrimage. For the first time in my career as a fan, I left a Jays game early but only because three rain delays had caused the game to drag on and I needed the rest, since I was one of the designated drivers for the Cooperstown excursion and my group wanted to be on its way early Saturday morning. And indeed, by 6:00 a.m. we were starting along the now familiar route I had used for my 1986 trip. Along the way, on Route 28 south, I again marvelled at the beautiful countryside. Everything seemed as lush and verdant as on my first drive through the area a year earlier. I looked forward not only to seeing Cooperstown and the Hall of Fame once again but also to seeing the glints of sunshine on the Canadarago Lake and the sign posted on the tree, indicating that we were once again in the Village of Fly Creek.

Upon our arrival in Cooperstown, I took the group through virtually the same tour I had made in 1986: the Chamber of Commerce office, Doubleday Field, the Hall of Fame building, Cooper Park, the Otesaga Hotel. Some of us attempted to get in the autograph line at the Otesaga for the Saturday afternoon session but unfortunately, the quota of two hundred persons had been met earlier in the day. As was the case with my first pilgrimage, some people had been in the queue since early Friday evening.

Sunday the 26th of July started early. By 7:00 a.m. my friends and I had staked out a claim on a prime vantage spot in Cooper Park, complete with lawn chairs and blankets spread on the lawn. Other members of our group joined us around 11:00 o'clock and we took turns going for breakfast, purchasing souvenirs and visiting the Hall of Fame. My morning was hectic: breakfast at the Short Stop restaurant; purchasing Induction Day Covers and having them cancelled at the Post Office; a short visit - one of several I would make during the weekend - to the Hall of Fame.

I had just come out of the Hall of Fame when a limousine pulled up beside the entrance. An Hall of Fame employee stepped out and assisted a frail, bespectacled, elderly gentleman out of the limousine. The distinguished gentleman declined an offer of further assistance and, aided by a black cane, slowly made his way on the sidewalk towards the entrance to Cooper Park. I quickened my pace and caught up with him. As I drew abreast of him, I realized he was James "Cool Papa" Bell whom I had seen at the Induction Ceremonies the previous year.

It took a few moments for the full impact of his presence to hit me. There I was, close to the man who was reputedly the fastest ball player ever to run the bases. I greeted him, "Hello! Mr. Bell. How do you do Sir?" He replied but I was too excited to catch what he said. I then turned to the people around us and said, "Folks, we are honoured to have among us "Cool Papa" Bell." Immediately, a crowd gathered around him, keeping at a respectful distance. Someone mentioned his blazing speed to which he remarked that that was a long time ago. Despite having lost most of his sight, Bell did sign a Hall of Fame postcard of himself for me - I had to guide his hand. He then distributed "cut"[1] autographs to about a dozen of us.

I returned to Cooper Park and engaged in conversation with the people around me, many faces now familiar from my 1986 visit to the Induction Ceremonies. I exchanged addresses with my fellow pilgrims and took some photographs with my off-season acquisition, a zoom lens camera. I had decided to buy a new camera after the 1986 Induction Ceremonies when my instamatic camera proved inadequate for pictures of the Hall of Famers on the platform, over thirty yards away.

---

1.   *The term "cut" autographs refers to small strips of paper which Bell had cut and upon which he had signed his name. The autographs had been prepared years earlier, while Bell's sight was still good.*

James "Cool Papa" Bell - 1987

41

At 2:30 p.m., Master of Ceremonies and President of the Baseball Writers' Association of America Gerry Fraley, opened the Induction. ESPN's George Grande then introduced the returning Hall of Famers. Of the fifty-seven members of the Hall still living, including the three to be inducted, twenty-eight were in attendance. To thunderous applause, these giants of the baseball world took their places on the platform - Stan Musial, Monte Irvin, Ralph Kiner, Enos Slaughter, Charlie Gehringer, Willie Mays, Robin Roberts, "Happy" Chandler, Rick Ferrell, "Cool Papa" Bell, Vernon "Lefty" Gomez, "The Big Cat", Johnny Mize, Warren Spahn, Bill Dickey, Ernie Banks, Lou Boudreau, Ted Williams, Roy Campanella, Joe Sewell, Judy Johnson, Bobby Doerr, "Pee Wee" Reese, Al Lopez, Bob Lemon and "Jocko" Conlan. A tinge of disappointment passed through me as I wondered why the other twenty-nine members did not attend. Were there perhaps some Hall of Famers who did not fully appreciate how dear they were to the hearts of the fans, near deities to tens of millions? I remembered Al Kaline who said at his 1980 induction: "I plan to return here when it is quiet, after the crowds have gone.... I also intend to come back every summer for each new induction to welcome the "rookies". (Voices from Cooperstown (New York: Collier Books, MacMillan Publishing Company), 1982. (p. 284.)

Prayers, a silent tribute to those baseball people who had moved on to a higher playing field, the singing of the National Anthem and a welcome address by the Mayor of Cooperstown, preceded the presentation of the media awards. The J. G. Taylor Spink Award for 1986 was presented to Jack Lang whose long career as a journalist included several prestigious positions: President of the New York Chapter of the Baseball Writers' Association of America (BBWAA), Secretary-Treasurer of the BBWAA, member of the Scoring Rules Committee of Major League Baseball. Lang worked with the Long Island Press for over thirty years then with the New York Daily News. He witnessed the arrival of Jackie Robinson in Brooklyn and covered the great Brooklyn Dodgers and the New York Yankee teams. He also covered the New York Mets, from their faltering beginnings to their World Championship years.

Jack Buck, the recipient of the Ford C. Frick Award, shared duties with Harry Caray before becoming principal broadcaster for the St. Louis Cardinals. Known as the "Voice of the Redbirds", Buck's distinguished career dated back to his days as a student at Ohio State University where he covered basketball and football. Following jobs with Cardinals' farm teams in

Columbus and Rochester he moved to radio station KMOX in St. Louis, eventually becoming the station's director. The versatile Buck has broadcast Super Bowl games and hosted NBC's "Grandstand".

Special invitees, the President of the Hall of Fame Ed Stack and Baseball Commissioner Peter Ueberroth, were introduced next. Ueberroth then took control of the dedication of the plaques. Ray Dandridge was first up. Selected by the Veterans' Committee, Dandridge played in the Negro Leagues, Cuba, Puerto Rico, Venezuela and also in the farm system of Major League Baseball. A slick fielding third baseman for most of his career, he regularly batted over .300. In 1940, he won the Mexican League batting crown with an average of over .370, and was the first black player to win the American Association MVP award, doing so in 1950 while he was the team-mate of an emerging star, Willie Mays. They were playing for the Minneapolis Millers, the AAA farm team of the New York Giants. In an emotional acceptance speech, Dandridge expressed gratitude for his selection and ended by thanking the baseball establishment for letting him "smell the roses".

Jim "Catfish" Hunter was the next to receive his plaque. The Commissioner touched on the highlights of Hunter's career. A major leaguer for fifteen seasons, Hunter played for the Kansas City Athletics, the Oakland Athletics and the New York Yankees. Among his accomplishments are five consecutive seasons with 20 or more wins, a perfect game and the 1974 Cy Young Award. "Catfish" was a member of the dominant Oakland Athletics teams of the early 1970's. Arm trouble cut short his career at age thirty-three. In accepting his plaque, Hunter traced his career in the majors, giving special thanks to former Oakland A's owner Charles Finley and to George Steinbrenner, owner of the New York Yankees.

Commissioner Ueberroth next presented Billy Williams with his plaque. In a major league career that lasted for over sixteen years, mainly with the Chicago Cubs, Billy Williams' record was impressive. Playing mostly in the outfield, he held the National League record for most consecutive games played, 1,117, at the time of his retirement. His other achievements include selections as National League Rookie of the Year (1961) and National League and Major League Player of the year (1972), selected by The Sporting News. He led the National League in slugging percentage (.606 in 1972), led the National League in total bases on three occasions and won a batting title, hitting .333 in 1972. Williams hit 426 home runs in the Major Leagues.

In accepting his plaque, Williams not only thanked the writers for electing him to the Hall of Fame but also rapped the knuckles of the baseball establishment for the lack of opportunities at the managerial and other higher echelons of baseball, for blacks and other minorities. The Master of Ceremonies then declared the proceedings over.

We returned to our motel shortly after the ceremonies were concluded, somewhat exhausted but very pleased by the day's events. Around midnight, one of my friends and I returned to Cooperstown. After parking behind the Chamber of Commerce office, we walked to the Otesaga hotel where, at 2:00 a.m., we joined the autograph line on the sidewalk outside the Otesaga Hotel. Over one hundred persons were already camped out ahead of us. We settled into sleeping bags and used blankets for added insulation from the cold night air that blew from across nearby Lake Otsego.

For most of the remainder of the night, we talked with our fellow pilgrims. Before I drifted off to sleep, I mused over the fact that I was camping overnight to obtain autographs. On numerous occasions, I had observed young men and women waiting in line overnight to buy concert tickets and considered them mad fools for exposing themselves to the elements. Yet here I was, forty-six years old, lying on a sidewalk in order to collect a few autographs.

It seemed as though I had been asleep for only a few minutes when I was awakened by the voice of the security guard. We were asked to register at the entrance to the chute through which we would eventually proceed to the autograph area. The autograph session was scheduled for 9:00 a.m. to 10:00 a.m. All one hundred and seventy-five of those allowed into the chute were registered by 6:30 a.m. I was #140. Several hundred were turned away during the night and in the early morning.

Around 7:00 a.m., Ted Williams, clad in a jogging suit, appeared and motioned for someone to bring him a chair. He sat beside the picket fence that formed the left side of the chute and gave us his autograph. "The Splendid Splinter" had an appointment that conflicted with the autograph session. Rather than disappoint fans, he chose to sacrifice his rest. After signing for an hour and with about twenty-five fans still in line for his autograph, Williams indicated that it was time for him to leave. A youngster exclaimed, "Aw!

Please Mr. Williams." Instead of leaving, "Teddy Ballgame" continued signing until everyone had an autograph. I thought, 'What a selfless gesture. How better to obtain the autograph of an Hall of Famer.' "Colonel" Dave Egan[1] must have turned in his grave. We dispersed to await the official signing session.

After breakfast and a quick visit to Doubleday Field, we returned to the Otesaga. The Hall of Famers were seated at two long tables. Since fans could choose only one table, my friend and I took separate lines. There were only six immortals seated along the table that I chose. Johnny Mize was first to sign, then Robin Roberts and Ralph Kiner. "Happy" Chandler was next. Just as the fan ahead of me reached Chandler, the former Commissioner was served breakfast - toast and tea. We waited patiently as Chandler broke pieces of toast which he dipped in the tea before eating. It was a moving experience. Here was a man who, as a Senator, as Governor of Kentucky and Baseball Commissioner, had once exercised so much power. Now at age eighty-nine, he was like a little child, soaking his toast before eating it. The scene brought to mind the saying, "once a man, twice a child".

Presently, Chandler finished his breakfast and resumed signing. He signed my book "A.B. Chandler". I moved on saying, "Thank you for what you did for baseball Sir." I was of course, referring to his role in enabling Jackie Robinson to break the colour barrier which had existed since the 1880's. As if he knew what I meant, he called me back, took my autograph book and added the words, "every good wish," above his signature. I then got "Catfish" Hunter's autograph, shook hands with him and moved over to the last member of the group, Bob Lemon. It was a wonderful feeling to be so close to so many baseball heroes. To me those men were larger than life: they were not ordinary mortals.

Having obtained our autographs, we wandered around Cooperstown until it was time for the Hall of Fame game at Doubleday Field, where we watched the New York Yankees beat the Atlanta Braves 3 - 0. We left Cooperstown at 5:30 p.m. and I arrived home at 1:30 a.m. on Tuesday. It had been a most rewarding and enjoyable weekend but little did I realize that I would soon again be visiting my Mecca.

---

1.   *Dave Egan, nicknamed "The Colonel", was a columnist for the Boston Daily Record. He was one of Williams'*
harshest critics and had accused Williams of being selfish and "not a team man". Egan's mean-spiritedness even
extended to Williams' last game in Boston. When Egan heard that the day had been declared "Ted Williams Day",
he wrote "Why are they having a day for THIS guy?"

CHAPTER VI

"THERE'S MORE TO COOPERSTOWN..." -
- Paul Fenimore Cooper, (Jr)
THE AUTUMN OF 1987

Shortly after I returned from Cooperstown, I made plans with my brothers and other relatives and friends to go back in late October. I wanted to visit the Hall of Fame at a time when there would be no crowd, a quieter time when I could be in true communion with my baseball heroes. I wanted also to compare the experience of going through the Hall at such a time with the experiences I had during the hectic Induction weekends.

Meanwhile, I wrote to former Commissioner, "Happy" Chandler, urging him to write about the part he played in the integration of baseball. I was delighted when Chandler replied to my letter and thanked me for my encouragement. He assured me that he was indeed working with his biographer on a book about "The Life and Times of Albert Benjamin Chandler". He said my words "warmed his heart", and sent me an autographed postcard of his Hall of Fame plaque.

Chandler's tenure as Commissioner lasted from 1945 to 1951. In 1946, Brooklyn Dodgers owner Branch Rickey, signed Jackie Robinson to a baseball contract and assigned him to the Dodgers' Triple A farm team, the Montreal Royals (Canada), of the International League. Rickey's goal was to break baseball's colour barrier, to enable blacks and other visible minorities to play in the Major Leagues. Rickey kept Robinson in Montreal awaiting the opportune moment to place him on the Dodgers' roster. But for Albert Benjamin Chandler, Jackie Robinson or any other black might not have played Major League baseball. At a meeting in early 1947, fifteen of the sixteen team owners voted against integration in the Majors: the sole "yes" vote was, of course, that of Branch Rickey. "Happy" Chandler refused to acknowledge this overwhelming vote and authorized Robinson's transfer to the Brooklyn Dodgers. In April 1947, Jackie Robinson made his debut with the Dodgers. Other clubs soon followed Brooklyn's example and began accepting blacks. Some, however, resisted for a considerable length of time and it took twelve years from the advent of Jackie Robinson for blacks to be included on all the Major League rosters.

"Happy" Chandler's defiance was not taken kindly and in large measure, contributed to the owners' refusal to renew his contract as Commissioner. It took thirty-five years from the time Chandler approved Robinson's entry for the baseball establishment to accord Chandler his rightful place among baseball's immortals. In 1982, a few months before his eighty-fourth birthday, Chandler was chosen for enshrinement into the Hall of Fame.

I had scarcely had time to add Chandler's letter to my growing collection before leaving for my second trip of the year to Cooperstown. On Friday, October 23, 1987, accompanied by my brother Neville and his wife, I set out. The weather was overcast, damp and chilly. In contrast to the vast continuous stretch of lush green vegetation - grass, shrubs and trees - that characterized the scenery during the drive to Cooperstown in the summer, the scene was now dull and dreary. Except for the occasional clump of evergreens, trees and plants were devoid of foliage. Bare greyish branches and shrivelled, brown grass made for a depressing drive along Highway 5 and Route 28. My spirits were somewhat boosted however, by the thought of the Hall of Fame and my loved ones in Cooperstown.

We arrived at our destination - the Mohican motel on Chestnut street - a few minutes before 10:00 p.m. We registered then called on the others in our party who had checked in earlier in the evening and who were all assembled in one of the larger rooms to await our arrival. We greeted one another warmly and discussed plans for the weekend. At one point in the evening, my brother Wally brought out the five books that comprise James Fenimore Cooper's Leatherstocking Tales - The Pioneers, The Last of the Mohicans, The Prairie, The Pathfinder and The Deerslayer. I surprised him by displaying four of the books which I had acquired - the fifth was out of stock. Unbeknown to each other, we had bought the same books to reacquaint ourselves with the area and the characters about whom Cooper had written.

Early on Saturday morning, we began our tour of the Village, covering Doubleday Field, Lake Front Park, Farmers' Museum and Fenimore House. I acted as tour guide, drawing attention to points of interest such as Council Rock and the Otesaga Hotel. The Otesago Boat Tours season was over so I gave a brief talk on the Otsego from the pier where the tours commence. The main attraction was, of course, the National Baseball Hall of Fame and Museum. Much of our time was, therefore, spent exploring the wonders within its walls.

FENIMORE HOUSE - FALL (1987)

49

It was scarcely three months since I had last walked through those hallowed halls and lovingly gazed upon the numerous artifacts and other displays, imbibing information in the process. Now I was about to do so once again, this time unencumbered by the crowd like that which fills the Hall during the Induction weekend. Only a few hardy fans were going through the turnstiles on this dull, wet autumn Saturday.

As I had done on previous occasions, I left the best - the main floor - for last. Starting on the second floor, I went through the exhibits, working systematically until all the displays were covered. I followed this pattern on all levels of the building. The trickle of visitors afforded me more time to concentrate on particular items. There was no pressure to move on, to make way for others.

I finally entered the Hall of Fame Gallery. The air of reverence that pervaded the room on my other visits was again evident and in this chamber as in the rest of the building, I experienced the same pure joy and thrill as before. Earlier, on my way to the Hall of Fame, I wondered whether this feeling would be diminished because of the number of visits I had made and especially in view of the fact that I was there only three months ago. All doubt was dispelled once I entered the Hall. Indeed, I felt greater respect and admiration after this visit. The sheer volume of artifacts and information coupled with the continued flow of new acquisitions ensure that the Hall of Fame and Museum will never cease to be a source of marvel and enjoyment to visitors. Three new plaques representing, Billy Williams, "Catfish" Hunter and Ray Dandridge - the latest inductees - were added to the wall, bringing to one hundred and ninety-nine, the number of immortals enshrined.

After what must have seemed an eternity to my relatives and friends, I emerged from the Hall of Fame Gallery and joined them in the gift shop where we purchased souvenirs. The cars were in Doubleday Park. On our way there along Main street we stopped by several stores and bought more baseball mementos. While I was awaiting some members of our group, I struck up a conversation with a gentleman lounging on one of the black wrought iron benches located along the Main street sidewalks. His name was Bill Adsit. A resident of Cooperstown, Adsit had been a pharmacist at the Church and Scott drugstore on Main and Pioneer streets but was now retired, having handed over the business to his sons.

Adsit talked about his love for baseball, of watching the Hall of Fame and Museum grow over the years, and of his friendship with the Busch Family, owners of the St. Louis Cardinals. He also spoke of a World Series ring given him as a souvenir by the Buschs. He enquired about my origins and how I became interested in baseball, and in particular, the Hall of Fame. We chatted for about twenty minutes and exchanged addresses. Before I took leave of Adsit, I asked him if there were any descendants of the Cooper family still residing in the Village. He informed me that a great-great-grand-daughter (a Mrs. Weil), and a great-great grandson (Paul Cooper), were indeed living in Cooperstown. I thanked him and caught up with my group.

Late on Saturday afternoon I obtained a copy of the Cooperstown telephone directory and found a listing for "Cooper". I called the number and spoke with Paul Cooper. I introduced myself, pointing out that I had read the Leatherstocking Tales as a young man in Guyana and asked if he would oblige by autographing our copies of the books. Cooper replied that he would be delighted to do so and we arranged to meet at his place at 10:00 am the next day.

At 9:15 o'clock on Sunday morning we left the Mohican motel for our visit with Paul Cooper. We drove north on Chestnut street and turned right into Susquehanna Avenue, headed for Bowerstown, just outside Cooperstown. Following directions given me the previous day, we continued on Susquehanna Avenue, crossed a bridge over the Susquehanna river until we came to a point where the road split into two, a few yards from the bridge. We took the left hand fork and presently arrived at our destination.

Paul Cooper and his mother lived in a quaint white house mostly hidden from the road by a hedge, trees and shrubs that bedecked the yard. They greeted us cheerfully and Cooper took us to a small building behind the house, a building that served as his study. Books, documents and posters were strewn all over the place - on desks, chairs, shelves and the floor. From a vast collection, he produced copies of several books and showed them to us. All were original hardcovers, signed by his great-great-grandfather.

During our exchange of information I learned that our host was a scholar who held a doctorate in Oceanography with emphasis on sea ice. He said he liked Canada, owned several acres of land in the Province of Alberta and once spent two years in the MacKenzie river delta in the Canadian North West Territories. Doctor Cooper was single and he appeared to be in his late forties. When I enquired what would become of his precious collection of books, he replied that he hoped to pass them to his brother's children.

After about thirty minutes, Dr. Cooper autographed our books. He signed mine as follows:

> *"With best wishes*
> *to Rudi (sic) Gafur*
> *from*
> *Nick Cooper*
> *or Paul Fenimore Cooper, Jr.*
> *great-great-grandson of*
> *the author of this."*

He also gave me two autographed posters depicting the arctic ocean covered with ice, taken from the air. His mother invited us for tea but we were anxious to get home so we thanked the Coopers and set out to join the relatives and friends awaiting us in Doubleday Park. As we walked to our car, Dr. Cooper made a poignant observation. He said, "you know Rudy after you 'phoned yesterday, my mother and I talked about your request for the autographs. It is refreshing to know that of the tens of thousands of people who come to Cooperstown every year someone (meaning me) realized that there is more to Cooperstown (meaning the Cooper family), than the Baseball Hall of Fame." I mumbled thanks and turned away so that no one could see my moist eyes. We met the rest of the group, said our goodbyes and took our separate ways home. Around 4:00 pm I arrived home, after yet another wonderful visit to Cooperstown. It seemed that my love for my baseball Mecca got stronger with each visit.

CHAPTER VII

WILVER AND KEN - NOVEMBER 1987 TO AUGUST 1988

Buoyed by the euphoria of my visit to Cooperstown, I looked closer to home for more baseball nurturing. In August, I had applied for membership as a patron of the fledgling Canadian Baseball Hall of Fame and Museum (CBHF&M), located in Toronto. Concerned after a three-month delay in hearing about my application, I arranged a meeting with the President of the CBHF&M, Bruce Prentice. I found out that there was a shortage of manpower and offered my services. Prentice asked me to co-ordinate the various activities of volunteers. I gladly agreed, setting in motion a period of very fruitful involvement in the operations of the CBHF & M.

Meanwhile, I wrote to the Director of the National Baseball Hall of Fame and Museum in Cooperstown and congratulated him for another well-organized Induction Weekend (1987); I also wrote and thanked Bill Adsit for his assistance and encouragement, and Paul Cooper for autographing the books, and for his kind sentiments. The Hall of Fame Director Howard Talbot, replied and thanked me for my support; Bill Adsit sent me a package containing numerous clippings on the Hall of Fame dating back to the first Induction Ceremonies in 1939. Bill had carefully preserved these precious items for fifty years. This gesture touched me deeply. In showing such confidence in me, a virtual stranger, Bill not only reinforced my faith and trust in humanity but also displayed a willingness to assist in the baseball education of a fellow devotee of the National Pastime and the Hall of Fame.

More good news followed. Toronto Blue Jays left fielder George Bell was named the American League's Most Valuable Player, the first player from a Canadian team and also the first from the Dominican Republic to be accorded the honour. In early January, the results of the voting by the Baseball Writers' Association of America were announced. Willie Stargell was chosen for enshrinement. On March 1, the eighteen-member Baseball Hall of Fame Committee on Baseball Veterans announced that it was unable to elect a candidate to the Hall of Fame: no one from a group that included Leo Durocher, Phil Rizzuto, and Tony Lazzeri had received the required 75 percent of the votes cast.

A month earlier, on February 4, I had written the outline of what would eventually result in this book. A few weeks later I started in earnest to organize volunteer activity at the Canadian Hall of Fame. As I updated the list of volunteers, I added ten more names - friends whom I had persuaded to join the cause. The range of activities at the Canadian Hall was vast: committees were established to do research, filing and cataloguing; walls were painted and exhibits re-arranged; volunteers were scheduled to oversee games, sell merchandise and work as security guards. I led a group of five liaising with a committee of officials from Beachville[1], Ontario. The first recorded baseball game in Canada was played in Beachville in 1838 and the CBHF&M asked local officials to assist in planning a number of activities to observe the Sesquicentennial of baseball in Canada.

In March, I went to Florida for Spring Training. Prior to leaving, I had written to seventeen Hall of Famers seeking their autographs, enclosing index cards and stamped, self-addressed envelopes. Most of my requests were honoured. A few asked for payment and while I have an aversion to paying for autographs, I decided to make an exception in the case of Edd Roush. My spring training itinerary included a Blue Jays/Pirates game in Bradenton where Mr. Roush lived. I had hoped to secure his autograph while I was there for the game but unfortunately, Mr. Roush died a few days prior to my arrival in Florida, two months shy of his ninety-fifth birthday.

The start of the season grew closer. In mid-April, the Canadian Baseball Hall of Fame and Museum held its annual fund-raising dinner with former Major League umpire Ron Luciano as the key-note speaker. As part of my continuing work with the local Hall of Fame, I dealt with membership-related activities. I set as my first task clearing the backlog of applications that still awaited processing, a backlog which, ironically, included my own application. I took care of these and offered to work on renewals which had been left unattended since the inception of the Canadian Hall of Fame but Bruce Prentice informed me he would deal with the matter.

And of course, by April, "the season" had started and among all my other activities, I found time to attend all Blue Jays home games, as well the annual

---

1.   *Beachville, population 800, is located in southwestern Ontario, about 100 miles from Toronto.*

reception sponsored by the Toronto Maple Leaf Baseball Club to start off its season. Cooperstown immortals, Bob Feller, Warren Spahn and Enos Slaughter together with baseball greats Don Newcombe, Lew Burdette, Larry Doby and Bobby Shantz, participated in the 1988 edition of this function.

I was now spending an increasing amount of time planning for the 1988 Hall of Fame Induction Ceremonies in Cooperstown, as well as a trip to the All-Star game in Cincinnati. The Induction Ceremonies would be very special indeed, as there almost were no Ceremonies for 1988. The Baseball Writers' Association of America had a list of forty-five candidates to consider for entry into the Hall. Only Wilver Dornel Stargell received the 75 % of the votes required for election and thus became the seventeenth person elected in his first year of eligibility and the two hundredth member selected for enshrinement. I drafted itineraries and reserved accommodation and tickets. I wrote to several of my friends, "the Cooperstown faithful", to share my plans. One day at a ball game, a fellow Blue Jays fan Grenville Bray, gave me a photograph taken in the 1940's. It featured Connie Mack, Chief Bender and Dick Fowler. Fowler pitched a no-hitter for the Athletics against the Browns in 1945, the only Canadian to do so in the Major Leagues. He was inducted into the Canadian Hall of Fame in 1985. I passed the photograph to Bruce Prentice for display in the Canadian Hall of Fame.

At dawn on Saturday, July 9, accompanied by friends from Sarnia, I left for Cincinnati and the All-Star game. We attended a regular season match-up between the Phillies and the Reds as well as the Equitable Old-Timers' game on Sunday. Heavy rainfall washed out the All-Star workout and other inter-league competition on Monday but we were able to get autographs of players at their hotel. It was a worthwhile trip, as we got to watch the American League squad win the Classic, 2-1. We broke up the trip home to Toronto with stops in Chicago and St. Louis.

It seemed as though I had just unpacked my suitcases from my Cincinnati/Chicago/St. Louis trip when it was time for my yearly pilgrimage to Cooperstown. On Saturday, July 30, accompanied by my younger son and my grandson, I set out for Cooperstown, collecting a couple of friends en route. We took the familiar route - Highway 401 east with connecting highways to Utica. After checking into our motel, we continued our journey to Cooperstown, arriving shortly after 2:00 p.m. Along the way, I pointed out the now familiar points of interest, including Fly Creek where the Doubleday baseball was found all those years ago among the belongings of Abner Graves.

Upon our arrival in Cooperstown, we tried to register for the autograph session scheduled for 3:30 p.m. that day at the Otesaga Hotel, hoping to be among the two hundred persons allowed in line for autographs by Hall of Fame members. We were too late. Registration had already taken place earlier in the day and the quota had been met by mid-morning, filled by people who had begun to line up early Friday evening. We toured the Village briefly and visited the Hall of Fame.

While the others spent time going through the entire Hall, I decided to concentrate on one section as I like to view the exhibits in a leisurely fashion. I had discovered from my previous visits that I needed more than one day to cover the Hall at my own pace. By taking the exhibits in sections over the weekend, I would be able to cover the Hall as well as attend the Induction Ceremonies, buy souvenirs and visit with friends like the Adsits. I spent about an hour on the second floor, viewing with interest the sections on *Black Baseball and The Evolution of Equipment* before turning to the displays about famous names in the game. I paid particular attention to the display of my favourite player, Ty Cobb, as well as those on Cy Young and Casey Stengel. From the Hall, I went to a card show on Railroad Avenue, where I bought copies of a baseball card newspaper <u>Tuff Stuff</u>, the cover of which featured Toronto Blue Jays rookie catcher, Pat Borders.

An autograph session for children was scheduled for 10:30 a.m. on Sunday and I had hoped to get my nine year old grandson Dairl into that session. However, ensuring a place for the session meant getting Dairl into the line on the sidewalk outside the Otesaga by 10:00 p.m. on Saturday. I quickly abandoned that idea when severe thunderstorms hit the area during the evening.

As Sunday dawned, my party was on its way from Utica to Cooperstown for the main event, the Induction Ceremonies. When we got there, about fifty persons were already gathered in Cooper Park, dotted around the green picket fence which set the special guests apart from the rest of the fans. We picked a suitable vantage point and took turns guarding the spot while the others had breakfast, toured the Village and shopped for souvenirs. I spent about an hour after breakfast in my favourite chamber, the Hall of Fame Gallery, going through the plaques of my heroes. Although I had passed through the Gallery several times before, I still felt the same power that gripped me on previous occasions. I devoted more time to the lesser known but equally deserving residents of the Hall, men like Jesse Burkett, Tim Keefe, James O'Rourke, John Montgomery Ward, and Bobby Wallace. I left the chamber with renewed vigour and enthusiasm, brought about by the happiness derived from my communion with my heroes.

By the time I returned to our "base of operations" in Cooper Park, the crowd had swelled to several thousand. I spotted many familiar faces, my fellow pilgrims from previous years. I greeted them briefly and promised to spend more time with them after I had attended to my usual Induction Day business. I then hurried off to the Main Street sidewalk to buy souvenirs and photographs of Hall of Famers. On my way back to Cooper Park, I collected a copy of the Induction Day Programme, the forty-ninth annual programme, courtesy of The Sporting News.

Returning to the Induction Grounds, I sought out friends with whom I had kept in touch since the last Induction Ceremonies and passed the time with them until the start of the ceremonies. It was like a family reunion as we exchanged gifts and brought each other up to date on baseball news from our respective areas. At 2:30 pm Master of Ceremonies Vern Plagenhoff, (President of the Baseball Writers' Association of America), declared the proceedings open. He then turned the microphone over to George Grande who introduced the returning Hall of Fame members. A few career highlights accompanied the announcement of each name. One by one, unhurriedly, they came up the platform, acknowledged the worshippers and took their seats on both sides of the dais.

Twenty-five of the immortals graced the ceremonies welcoming Willie Stargell into baseball's Pantheon: "Jocko" Conlan, Lou Boudreau, "Lefty" Gomez, Ray Dandridge, George Kell, Billy Williams, Johnny Mize, "Buck" Leonard, Billy Herman, Ted Williams, "Cool Papa" Bell, "Happy" Chandler, Bob Lemon, "Pee Wee" Reese, Stan Musial, Monte Irvin, Robin Roberts, Enos Slaughter, Roy Campanella, Willie McCovey, Charlie Gehringer, Ernie Banks, Warren Spahn, Bill Terry and Ralph Kiner. I took photographs as they came to the front of the stage.

Presentation of the media awards to Jim Murray and Lindsey Nelson led up to the Dedication itself. Murray was the recipient of the 1987[2] J. G. Taylor Spink award, given for *"for meritorious contributions to baseball writing"*. Murray won numerous honours for his excellent writing, among them "America's Best Sportswriter" (fourteen times); the "Headliners Award" (twice) and the Associated Press Sports Editors Association citation for best sports column. Murray worked with the <u>New Haven Register,</u> the <u>Los Angeles Examiner,</u> <u>Time Magazine</u> and <u>Sports Illustrated,</u> moving to the <u>Los Angeles Times</u> in 1961. Murray's column, which appears in the <u>Times</u> and is syndicated in newspapers all over the U.S., is well known for consistently evoking the gamut of readers' emotions. As well, Murray's style and candour have earned him the respect and admiration of his colleagues who regard him as the dean of columnists.

Lindsey Nelson received the Ford C. Frick Award, for *"for major contributions to the game of Baseball"*. Nelson covered the New York Mets for seventeen years, from their fledgling days to their rise to prominence and beyond. After serving in the armed forces during World War II, Nelson worked minor league baseball games in Knoxville before graduating to bigtime broadcasting. He called basketball's "Game of the Week" for six years and NCAA football for fourteen years. A mainstay at the Cotton Bowl which he covered for twenty-six years, Nelson is also known for his flashy, multi-coloured sports jackets.

At last, the Commissioner of Baseball, Peter Ueberroth, rose to dedicate Willie Stargell's plaque. The Commissioner referred to the long and impressive career of Stargell, pointing out several highlights. These include Co-MVP of the National League (1979), <u>The Sporting News</u> Major League Player of the Year and Man of the Year (1979); National League Comeback Player of the Year (1978) and four-time member of <u>The Sporting News</u> National League All-Star Team. Known for his prodigious home run blasts, Willie hit 475 homers in a Major League career that spanned just over twenty years. In 1980, he was honoured for his work in fighting Sickle Cell Anaemia, receiving an honorary degree from St. Francis College in Loretto, Pennsylvania. Stargell, in accepting his plaque, thanked the members of the BBWAA, as well as the people who helped him along in his baseball career, including former Pirate manager

---

2.   *The winner of the Spink Award is honoured in the year following selection.*

Danny Murtaugh. The Master of Ceremonies then declared the proceedings closed.

I said goodbye to my friends and promised to keep in touch with them. We wandered around Cooperstown for a while, bought more souvenirs and returned to our motel in Utica for supper and a short rest before the second part of our day began. We had barely caught a couple of hours sleep when the alarm on my wristwatch woke us up. We left for Cooperstown around 10:15 p.m., intent on joining the line for the autograph session arranged for 9:00 a.m. on Monday. Arriving outside the Otesaga hotel a few minutes after 11:00 p.m., we learned that the two hundred-person quota had already been met. We drove back to Utica tired and deeply disappointed .

On Monday morning, we checked out of the motel and went back to Cooperstown. After breakfast the group split up, arranging to meet in Doubleday Park before the Hall of Fame game. I paid another visit to the Hall of Fame before setting out to meet my friend Bill Adsit who awaited me at the Church and Scott Pharmacy. Bill greeted me heartily and I was able to thank him in person for his trust, his friendship and his kindness toward me. As Bill and I talked about baseball and about Cooperstown, I learned more about the Village and about its affinity with the National Pastime and the Hall of Fame. In the course of our discussion, I mentioned that I had recently read an excellent book about the inauguration of the Hall of Fame, *Baseball's Hall of Fame*. Bill said he knew the author and asked if I would like to meet him. At first, I thought Bill was joking. I was sceptical that someone who had written about opening day, June 12, 1939 was still alive almost fifty years later but Bill assured me that the author was very much alive and lived nearby. Delighted at the prospect of meeting such a distinguished person, I accepted and we set out to meet Ken Smith, author of *Baseball's Hall of Fame*.

A ten-minute walk west on Main street and south on Chestnut street brought us to Glen Avenue. A few yards west on Glen and we were at our destination, the Protzman Nursing Home, now the residence for Ken Smith and his wife Emmie. Kenneth Danforth Smith started his long association with baseball as a batboy for his home town Danbury, Connecticut team in 1913. His coverage of major league baseball began with the New York Graphic in 1925. He moved to the New York Mirror in 1927 and covered the Giants for thirty years. When the Giants moved to San Francisco in 1958, Smith tried to go with them but a transfer could not be arranged so he turned to covering the New York Yankees. In 1963, he was appointed Director of the National Baseball Hall of Fame and Museum, stepping down in 1976 to accept the position as the Hall's Public Relations Director, a position he held until his retirement in 1979. Smith was also for many years Secretary-Treasurer of the Baseball Writers' Association of America.

On our way to the nursing home, Bill had explained to me that Ken was suffering from Alzheimer's disease, although I found Smith alert and articulate for most of our twenty minute visit with him. The three of us talked about his days as a reporter for the <u>New York Mirror</u>, covering the New York Giants. Smith made special note of his relationship with the ball players, especially with "The Meal Ticket", Carl Hubbell with whom he shared accommodation. Emmie brought out several old black and white photographs of Ken with the players and key baseball people of the era. Ken showed me his J. G. Taylor Spink Citation which he received in 1984 and much to my delight, capped off the visit by signing my autograph book. I took photographs of Ken, Emmie and Bill and we left.

As we left the Smiths, I felt profound sorrow over what I had just shared with Bill. I had visited a man with a once brilliant and incisive mind, a man who now resided in a nursing home, ravaged by an inexplicable illness that robbed him of his faculties. Smith was once a giant in the baseball community, respected by players and owners alike and admired by his peers in the media. Yet here he was now, reduced to a mere shell, virtually helpless and neglected, save for the occasional visitor. It was a painful and sad experience to see him in such condition and the fragile nature of good health hit home quite forcefully.

Sobered by those thoughts, I rejoined my group at Doubleday Park where we watched the Hall of Fame game between the Cubs and the Indians. The game ended in a 1 - 1 tie. Around 5:00 p.m., we departed for Canada. My weekend in Cooperstown reinforced the belief that I would never grow tired of visiting the Hall of Fame. Not only had I witnessed the Induction of one of my heroes, I had also met one of the legendary baseball scribes and a builder of the Hall of Fame, Ken Smith. My life was indeed enriched and I felt I was taking a part of Cooperstown with me to Canada, memories and experiences that would sustain me until it came time to return to my Mecca for renewal.

CHAPTER VIII

THE ANNIVERSARIES - Summer of 1988 to Summer of 1989

On my return, I plunged back into my volunteer work at the Canadian Baseball Hall of Fame and Museum, the glow of my pilgrimage to Cooperstown still very much with me. In August, the Hall sponsored the Canadian premiere of the movie *Eight Men Out*. The movie is a credible version of the banishment from baseball of eight Chicago White Sox players accused of throwing the 1919 World Series in return for payment from gamblers. Several people associated with the film attended, including Executive Producer Barbara Boyle, Author Eliot Asinof, D. B. Sweeney ("Shoeless" Joe Jackson) and John Cusack ("Buck" Weaver). The event was an overwhelming success and the movie itself was among the top box office draws for several weeks. The premiere was followed by the launching of a new postage stamp, a second successful event staged by the Canadian Hall of Fame. Canada Post issued the stamp to commemorate the Sesquicentennial of the first recorded baseball game played in Canada.

But the focus of my off-season was, as was rapidly becoming the norm, my preparations for the trip to Cooperstown. I started getting ready for the 1989 Induction Ceremonies in Cooperstown earlier than in previous years. Since 1989 was a year of great significance to the Hall of Fame, to baseball in general and also for Cooperstown itself, I felt that attendance at the Induction Ceremonies would inevitably be higher than usual. Nineteen eighty-nine was literally " The Year of the Anniversaries": the Golden Anniversary of the opening of the National Baseball Hall of Fame and Museum; the Sesquicentennial of the game supposedly organized by Abner Doubleday; the Bicentennial of the birth of Cooperstown's most famous citizen - James Fenimore Cooper. Moreover, with several popular players becoming eligible for election to the Hall in 1989, the attendance figures were guaranteed to soar, putting additional pressure on facilities such as accommodation. I circulated a letter to my friends during Blue Jays games, urging them to plan early if they were going to the Induction Ceremonies.

In late November, as I was drafting a letter to all the Hall of Famers regarding the 1989 Induction, I heard of the death of the "Meal Ticket", Carl Hubbell.

Bill Adsit told me later that Ken Smith, former baseball writer and Director of the Hall of Fame whom I had met during my 1988 pilgrimage, wept bitterly upon hearing of Mr. Hubbell's passing. Ken and "King" Carl were room-mates when Ken covered the Giants for the New York Mirror. I wrote to the members of the Hall of Fame, entreating them to make a special effort to attend the 1989 festivities. I did not expect replies but received a card from Bobby Doerr assuring me that he would be present.

On January 10, 1989 the results of the Hall of Fame voting were announced. The Baseball Writers' Association of America chose Carl Yastrzemski and Johnny Bench for enshrinement into the Hall of Fame. Canada's Ferguson Jenkins, on the ballot for the first time, placed fifth in the voting. My elation was dampened somewhat by news of the death, at age ninety, of Hall of Famer Bill Terry, the last National League player to hit .400, batting .401 in 1931. Less than two weeks later, Carl Furillo, the "Reading Rifle", died at the age of sixty-six. Furillo was one of Roger Kahn's famed "Boys of Summer"[1], one of "Dem Bums", as the famed Brooklyn Dodgers of the 40's and 50's were affectionately known to their fans. At the end of February, the Hall of Fame Veterans' Committee chose former umpire Al Barlick and Cardinals great Red Schoendienst for entry into the Hall. Earlier in the month Hall of Famer "Lefty" Gomez died at age eighty.

During the winter, I wrote to Ty Cobb's children, Beverly Cobb-McLaren, Shirley Cobb-Beckwith and James Cobb, asking to meet them during their visit to Cooperstown for the Induction Ceremonies. I sent each of them a copy of the letter I had written to the Governor of Georgia in 1985 as part of my campaign to have the centennial of Cobb's birth observed. Mrs. McLaren replied that she and her brother Jim would be attending the Ceremonies and hoped to meet me. I also got in touch with several of my friends in the United States, sending them packages of information that I prepared on Cooperstown and the Hall of Fame.

The season's opening game seemed closer as I spent a week watching the Blue Jays during spring training in Florida. While there, I was privileged to meet one of the giants of baseball broadcasting, Ernie Harwell. It was not long

---

1.   *Kahn, a former writer for the New York Herald Tribune, later wrote about Furillo and the other Dodgers in a book called The Boys of Summer. The book is regarded as a classic among baseball books and deals with the lives of the baseball players after their playing days were over.*

after I returned that the baseball season opened in early April. The Blue Jays played their home opener on Friday, April 14 and beat the Kansas City Royals 3-0. Despite the victory, there was an air of sadness at the park, for that game was the team's final home opener at Exhibition Stadium. The Stadium had been home to the Jays since their inception in 1977. The Jays were scheduled to move into their new quarters in June, 1989 and fans had fond memories of the old park, including Doug Ault's two home runs on that snowy first home opener in April, 1977; George Bell's catch for the final out on October 5, 1985 to give the Jays their first American League East title; Kelly Gruber's inside-the-park home run in the dense fog on June 12, 1986.

May was an eventful month for baseball in Canada. On May 1, the Canadian Hall of Fame held its annual fund-raising dinner. Willie Mays, Mickey Mantle and "Duke" Snider as well as Whitey Ford, the "Chairman of the Board", were the guests of honour. A week later on May 6, the Toronto Maple Leaf Baseball Club had its season-opening banquet. The head table comprised Johnny Sain, Luis Tiant, Hank Bauer, Dick Williams and Hall of Famers Enos Slaughter and Warren Spahn.

But the most significant event that May was the Toronto Blue Jays final game at Exhibition Stadium on the 29th. The "Mistake by the Lake" held many wonderful memories for me: it was there that I saw my first "live" baseball game; I had met many fine baseball fans and some very enduring relationships had their origins at that Stadium. As part of the final game coverage, I was featured, along with a few of my friends from the bleachers, in a front-page article in a local newspaper. Our opinions of baseball at Exhibition Stadium were mostly positive and terms such as nostalgia, camaraderie and fondness flowed freely. Fittingly, the Blue Jays won their last game at the old ball park by a score of 7-5 on a dramatic 10th inning two-run homer by George Bell. The Blue Jays moved to their brand new home base, the Skydome in Toronto where they played their first game on June 5.

At 2:00 a.m. on Saturday, June 10, I left Toronto for Cooperstown. Earlier, on Friday evening, I watched the Blue Jays defeat the Tigers 2-0 and rested for an hour after the game. I then picked up friends and started down the familiar route to Cooperstown. Rain and fog hampered our drive, and fatigue forced me to pull in to rest stops for short naps. Despite the delays, we arrived in Cooperstown around 12:00 noon, the day on which the Hall of Fame's Fiftieth

Anniversary celebrations were officially launched. We missed the parade which was part of the festivities but were in time to witness the ribbon-cutting ceremony for the opening of the Fetzer/Yawkey wing of the Hall of Fame. I visited the Hall of Fame for about an hour, bought souvenirs and spent some time with Bill Adsit at the Church and Scott premises. We then watched the Equitable Old Timers' game at Doubleday Field and returned home to Toronto.

Baseball history was created on June 27, when the Toronto Blue Jays played the Baltimore Orioles at Memorial Stadium. It was the first time in the Major Leagues that opposing managers - Cito Gaston for the Blue Jays and Frank Robinson for the Orioles - were blacks.

Ty Cobb's daughter Beverly McLaren wrote to say that she would be unable to make the trip to Cooperstown for the Induction Ceremonies as indicated earlier. She had attended the festivities on June 10, but informed me that her brother Jim would be in Cooperstown during the period and that she would "tell him to expect to see you". Mrs. McLaren told me where to locate her brother. What a very thoughtful gesture! I wrote and thanked her and also wrote to Jim expressing my thrill at the prospect of meeting him.

My pilgrimage for the Induction Ceremonies began earlier than usual this year. On Thursday, July 20, I started out with a couple of friends for my Mecca. After checking into a motel in Utica, we continued on our journey, arriving in Cooperstown around 1:00 p.m. I repeated the ritual that I had performed so many times before - taking two first-time pilgrims on an orientation of the Village. By now, I fancied myself somewhat of an expert and received the ultimate compliment from Bill Adsit who told me that I knew more about Cooperstown than some people who resided there. I gave gifts to Bill and to the Director of the Hall of Fame, Howard Talbot, and made a brief visit to the Shrine. I rejoined the others and we returned to Utica.

I was up and ready to leave the motel by 5:30 a.m. but my two companions, exhausted from the previous day's activities, required a little extra rest. We finally arrived in Cooperstown by 9:00 a.m. and went our separate ways, agreeing to meet at a designated spot later. I headed straight for the Hall of Fame, starting from the second floor. I had scarcely gone past the Ty Cobb exhibit, the second on this level, when I struck a conversation with an Hall of

Fame employee, conspicuous by the bright red blazer worn by certain staff members. The gentleman, Dave Fundis, a physical education teacher in Cooperstown, was working at the Hall during the Summer. We talked about baseball in general - he was an Orioles fan - and about the Hall of Fame in particular. He seemed genuinely interested in my conversion from cricket to baseball and my enthusiasm for the game and its history. I told Mr. Fundis that I was hoping to meet Jim Cobb later that day, adding that I revered Jim's illustrious father. Fundis indicated that he knew Jim Cobb and asked me to meet him after 1:00 p.m. at the Hall of Fame. I viewed exhibits for about an hour afterwards, bought souvenirs and visited Bill Adsit (Jr.) and his brother David at Church and Scott Pharmacy.

To fill in time, I made a quick trip to the motel where Jim Cobb was staying but he was out playing golf. I left a message saying that I would see him later and hastened back to the Hall to keep my appointment with Dave Fundis. As soon as he saw me, he motioned me to wait and left for a few minutes. Presently, he returned with a book which he handed to me, a copy of Ty Cobb's autobiography *My Life in Baseball - the True Record*. After examining it for a while, I offered it back to Dave with the comment that I would like to read it. He looked me in the eye and said, "It is yours to keep". I was speechless. Engulfed with emotion, I protested that I could not accept such a cherished family item, for while examining the book I had noticed the inscription *"In memory of Donald Burch, 1973, to Ross Fundis."* How could I take an heirloom that had belonged to Fundis' father? Dave would have none of my objections and urged it upon me, adding that he knew I would treasure it and put it to good use. There are not enough superlatives to describe how profoundly moved I was by this gesture. This extraordinarily generous man was giving me, a stranger whom he had met just a few hours earlier, a valued and sentimental article. Somewhat sheepishly, I accepted the gift, mumbled a few words of thanks and asked Dave to autograph it for me. While he was doing so I reached for a napkin, as it was difficult to restrain the tears that welled up in my eyes. Dave wrote, *"To Rudy Gafur; best wishes to an upbeat guy: Dave Fundis, July 21, 1989"*. He introduced me to another Cooperstown resident, Ron Visco with whom I exchanged addresses. I thanked my new benefactor once more, then joined my companions who were awaiting me at Doubleday Park.

I went to meet Jim Cobb accompanied by my friends. My luck held up: Jim

WITH JIM COBB, COOPERSTOWN - 1989

was at the motel. He greeted me effusively, saying he was expecting me. Cobb was a small man in his late sixties; he spoke softly, unhurriedly and in a friendly manner throughout our conversation. He enquired about my interest in his father and was quite pleased that Canadians knew about his father's exploits between the white lines. In turn, I learned that he was very fond of his father, and that contrary to opinions held in certain quarters, Ty Cobb had a good relationship with his children. Jim also told me that his father knew the names of the four baseball writers who had not voted for him at the time of his election to the Hall of Fame[2]. I showed him the book Dave Fundis had given me and asked him to autograph it for me. He did so willingly. I introduced him to my friends and we took photographs with him. I thanked him for his time and asked that he convey my regards to his sister Beverly.

I then took my travelling companions to the autograph registration area outside the gates of the Otesaga Hotel. We entered our names for a draw to determine who would be allowed into the autograph line on Saturday. Soon after we returned to Utica to rest for the big day.

Saturday, July 22

I had hoped to leave Utica for Cooperstown around daybreak that Saturday, as I had been accustomed to doing since my first trip in 1986. For the second day in a row, the others in my group were a little late getting started. I considered this a minor irritant, for my friends were not accustomed to the hectic pace with which I went about my business in Cooperstown. We finally reached the village at 12:30 p.m. and headed for the autograph registration centre to check if our names were drawn for the 3:30 p.m. session.

Two of us were successful. Reporting time was at 1:30 p.m., so we passed the hour chatting with other fans. Finally, the signing began. The immortals were divided into four groups. I had registered for the fourth group so I lined up and had two baseballs autographed, four signatures on each ball, by Al Barlick, Stan Musial, Brooks Robinson, Willie Stargell, Willie McCovey, Red Schoendienst, Enos Slaughter and Johnny Mize. I thanked each of the gentlemen and went in search of some of my fellow pilgrims who were due to arrive from different parts of the United States: New York, Maryland and

---

2.   *Cobb had received 222 of the 226 votes cast.*

Massachusetts. Over the next two hours I met several of my friends at various points and in each case, we exchanged greetings, hugged and kissed and traded information. I presented each family with a package of gifts from Canada: each package included a Canadian Baseball Hall of Fame programme, a Blue Jays scorebook/programme and a Blue Jays calendar.

I was expecting the rest of my party from Canada to arrive sometime on Saturday afternoon, so I got back to Utica by 6:30 p.m. to take them to Cooperstown for an orientation tour. They had, however, left the motel before I returned. I was not worried as some of the party were "returnees" and I had prepared detailed information - maps, routes and scenic highlights - for everyone.

Induction day, Sunday 23rd.

We were up and on our way by 5:30 a.m. arriving at Cooper Park a few minutes past 6:30 a.m. Even I, a Cooperstown veteran, was unprepared for the scene that awaited us. Scores of lawn chairs were chained all around the green picket fence erected to separate the special guests from the rest of the fans. Several hundred people were scattered throughout the Park and Yastrzemski and Bench T-shirts were everywhere. We camped several yards from the fence. At first I was a little perturbed at being relegated so far back, having been accustomed to standing next to the fence, a position that afforded a good vantage point for seeing the Hall of Famers and for taking photographs. I realized almost immediately that I was not viewing the situation objectively; these people had come to see their heroes anointed and take their rightful place among baseball's elite. They deserved their day in the sun and who was I to begrudge them that! Besides, this was probably the first visit for most of them and many would likely never come again.

I sought out my friends and found them spread out all over the grounds. While making my rounds, I ran into friends from Lewiston, Maine whom I had met at a ball game at Toronto's Exhibition Stadium in the mid - eighties. Members of my party from Canada and my U.S. friends whom I had seen on Saturday afternoon were all present and I learned later that other friends from Hamburg, New York were also among the crowd, but I missed seeing them. I carried out my now accustomed ritual while I awaited the start of the

INDUCTION DAY (1989): AL BARLICK, RED SCHOENDIENST, CARL YASTRZEMSKI, JOHNNY BENCH, BART GIAMATTI, ED STACK; (FRONT ROW): WILLIE McCOVEY, ENOS SLAUGHTER, WARREN SPAHN, MONTE IRVIN, "COOL PAPA" BELL; (SECOND ROW).

Induction Ceremonies: a brief visit to the Hall of Fame, my usual purchases –
cachets and other souvenirs, and collection of copies of the Fiftieth Annual
Programme.

The gathering had been growing steadily since I first arrived and by the
time the Ceremonies got underway, the Park was filled to overflowing. Over
fifteen thousand persons were present. The President of the Baseball Writers'
Association of America, Phil Pepe, was Master of Ceremonies. He made a few
opening remarks then yielded the microphone to George Grande who, with
his usual zest introduced the returning Hall of Fame members. Twenty-six
immortals came to welcome the four newly elected residents to the hallowed
institution.

To thunderous applause, we acknowledged our heroes as they came up the
platform and took their seats. A few career highlights accompanied the intro-
duction of each member. They were presented in the following order: Rick
Ferrell, Billy Herman, Willie Stargell, Bob Lemon, Bobby Doerr, Al Lopez,
"Duke" Snider, Willie McCovey, Enos Slaughter, Warren Spahn, Monte Irvin,
"Pee Wee" Reese, Ralph Kiner, "Cool Papa" Bell, Johnny Mize, Robin Roberts,
Harmon Killebrew, Billy Williams, Bob Feller, Joe Sewell, Roy Campanella,
Ernie Banks, Brooks Robinson, Stan Musial, Ted Williams and Charlie
Gehringer. Tears, sadness, laughter, admiration, wistfulness and excitement
filled the air. Cameras clicked and people jockeyed for positions to get a
glimpse of their baseball gods.

Prayers, a silent tribute to baseball people who had passed away since the
last Induction Ceremonies, the singing of the U.S. National Anthem and a welcome by the Mayor of Cooperstown followed on the agenda and then the
media awards were presented. Receiving the J. G. Taylor Spink Award for
baseball writing were Bob Hunter and Ray Kelly. Hunter wrote for the <u>Herald
Examiner,</u> the <u>Valley News</u> and the <u>Los Angeles Daily News</u>. He served as
Chairman of the Baseball Writers' Association of America and prepared the
script for the TV series "Double Play with Durocher Day", featuring Leo
Durocher and his wife Laraine Day. Ray Kelly died in 1988 and the Award was
accepted by his son Ray Kelly, Jr. Kelly worked for the <u>Philadelphia Evening
and Sun Bulletin</u>, covering the Athletics and later, the Phillies. He held the
post of President of the Baseball Writers' Association of America.

The Ford C. Frick Award for baseball broadcasting was given to Harry

INDUCTION DAY (1989): ROY CAMPANELLA, JOE SEWELL, CHARLIE GEHRINGER, DUKE SNIDER, BOB FELLER, TED WILLIAMS, BILLY WILLIAMS, STAN MUSIAL, BOBBY DOERR, BOB LEMON, BROOKS ROBINSON, ROBIN ROBERTS, WILLIE STARGELL, ERNIE BANKS, JOHNNY MIZE AND RICK FERRELL.

Caray. His broadcasting career started with the St. Louis Cardinals in 1944, a post he held for twenty - five years. He then spent a year with the Oakland A's and ten years with the White Sox before moving to the Cubs where he became a fixture. His trademark "Holy Cow" and his leading the fans in singing, "Take Me Out to the Ball Game" have made his name a household word in baseball circles.

Mr. Pepe then introduced the distinguished guests, Hall of Fame President Ed Stack and the Commissioner of Baseball, A. Bartlett Giamatti who took control of the Dedication of the Plaques. The first recipient was former major league umpire Al Barlick who was chosen by the Veterans' Committee. In a career that spanned 1940 to 1971, Barlick earned a reputation as a disciplinarian: he was a strict but fair arbiter. The sixth umpire to be invited to take up residence in baseball's Pantheon, Barlick worked during some of the sport's most dramatic and historic moments. He witnessed Enos Slaughter's dash from first to home in the 1946 World Series between the Cardinals and the BoSox. He was present on April 15, 1947 when Jackie Robinson played in his first game for the Brooklyn Dodgers, thereby ending the abhorrent system that had excluded blacks from the Major Leagues for over half a century. He saw "the" catch by Willie Mays in 1954.

Red Schoendienst, also selected by the Veterans' Committee was next in line. In a career that included nineteen years as a Major League ball player and over twelve years as a manager, Schoendienst was a model of dedication, perseverance and durability. He established or tied several National League records for second basemen, appeared in ten All-Star games and earned five world series rings. In addition to a career .289 batting average, Schoendinst had an outstanding managerial record of 1028 wins and 944 loses, including two first place and three second place finishes.

Catcher extraordinaire Johnny Bench, was honoured next. A major league player for seventeen seasons, Bench won many honours including National League Rookie of the Year (1968); National League Most Valuable Player (1970 & 1972); thirteen consecutive selections to the National League All-Star team; ten consecutive Gold Glove Awards for defensive excellence as a catcher; World Series MVP in 1976. A member of the Big Red Machine of the seventies, Bench spent his entire career with Cincinnati. Elected in his first year of eligibility, Johnny Bench was termed by ex-Reds manager Sparky Anderson, "the first great one-handed catcher."

The entrance to Doubleday Field

Finally, Mr. Giamatti dedicated the plaque of Carl Yastrzemski. Also elected in his first year of eligibility, Yastrzemski played for the Boston Red Sox for twenty - three seasons. He equalled or set seven American and Major League records and is the only American League player to get at least 3,000 hits (3,419) and 400 home runs (452), and the first player to get at least 100 hits every year for his first twenty seasons. Yastrzemski also won the Triple Crown in 1967, was named American League MVP that same year, was awarded seven Gold Gloves and was selected to seventeen All-Star games. As if that impressive list of accomplishments were not enough, Yastrzemski also led the League in assists by outfielders for seven years, a Major League record.

Each of the newly-anointed Hall of Fame members in turn made an acceptance speech, simple and short, almost lack-lustre in contrast to the previous years when the inductees gave spirited, sometimes moving, acceptance speeches. The 1989 Inductees thanked the people who assisted them during their careers, including their families, the Baseball Writers, Veterans' Committee members and the fans for their support. The Master of Ceremonies then thanked everyone for attending and brought the proceedings to a close. I was able to find a few of my friends in the massive crowd to say good-bye before my own travelling associates and I returned to our quarters in Utica.

We checked out of the motel mid-morning Monday and drove to Cooperstown. I visited the Shrine, looked for the four new inductees and said a silent goodbye to the heroes who reposed therein. I then went to Doubleday Field for the Hall of Fame game. The Cincinnati Reds were scheduled to play the Boston Red Sox but the Reds who were in Montreal, were unable to get a charter flight in time for the game. An intra-squad game between the BoSox and some players from their minor league system was played instead. During the game I made friends with another Cooperstown resident, Butch Deis who was working as an usher around the first base area.

I took leave of the Adsits and Dave Fundis, and left Cooperstown at 4:10 p.m.. On the way home, I reflected on the events of the weekend. I tried to compare this and previous visits with a view to determining how they ranked in terms of satisfaction. I discovered that was virtually impossible as each time was very different. To be sure, there were common elements to each visit: Doubleday Park, the boat cruise, the museums, the Hall of Fame. Yet my experiences, my contacts with other fans and with other special people were differ-

HALL OF FAME GAME DAY AT DOUBLEDAY FIELD; HALL OF FAME MEMBERS ARE INTRODUCED TO FANS.

ent on each occasion. How could I quantify the thrill of meeting "Cool Papa" Bell? Or witnessing "Happy" Chandler dip pieces of toast in his tea at the autograph table? Or talking with Ken Smith, or hearing Paul Cooper's touching comments? How could I quantify and rate such unique experiences? One fact of which I was absolutely certain however, was that I would never have enough of Cooperstown and the Hall of Fame. I would never get my fill of the Shrine and I would continue my pilgrimage to the end of my days. With that thought in mind, I set my course for home.

CHAPTER IX

O! CANADA
SEPTEMBER 1989 TO AUGUST 1991

Once back from Cooperstown, I settled into my routine of work and watching the Toronto Blue Jays who were in a stretch drive for the Divisional Championship. They eventually won the American League East, only to be overwhelmed by the Oakland Athletics in the League Championship Series. Later that fall, the Canadian Baseball Hall of Fame suffered a major setback when it was forced to vacate its space at Ontario Place. This meant transferring all the exhibits to storage where they remain up to the present, an exile of over five years. Officials have since been trying to find a new home. In the meantime, they have continued to operate on a limited scale by exhibiting items in shopping malls and other places.

The baseball world received a shock on Friday, September 1, 1989 with the news of the death of Commissioner A. Bartlett Giamatti at age fifty-one. I was talking with other fans by gate nine at the Skydome around 4:45 p.m. when Blue Jays broadcaster Tom Cheek came along and informed us that Mr. Giamatti had died of a heart attack. I was deeply affected by the news.

Giamatti was a baseball fan without peer and had an abiding love for the game. I remember reading his eloquent appeal for the end of the 1981 baseball strike, as well as his essay, *Green Fields of the Mind*, written in 1977 while Giamatti was President of Yale. This essay captures the very essence of what every fan experiences when the baseball season ends. It reads in part:

> *It breaks your heart. It is designed to break your heart. The game begins in the spring, when everything else begins again, and it blossoms in the summer, filling the afternoons and evenings, and then as soon as the chill rains come, it stops and leaves you to face the fall alone. You count on it, rely on it to buffer the passage of time, to keep the memory of sunshine and high skies above, and then just when the days are all twilight, when you need it most, it stops....*

> *Somehow, the summer seemed to slip by faster this time. Maybe it wasn't this summer, but all the summers that, ... slipped by so fast.*

There comes a time when every summer will have something of autumn about it. Whatever the reason, it seemed to me that I was investing more and more in baseball, making the game do more of the work that keeps time fat and slow and lazy. I was counting on the game's deep patterns, three strikes, three outs, three times three innings, and its deepest impulse, to go out and back, to leave and to return home, to set the order of the day and to organize the daylight....

Of course, there are those who learn after the first few times. They grow out of sports. And there are others who were born with the wisdom to know that nothing lasts .... I need to think something lasts forever, and it might as well be that state of being that is a game; it might as well be that, in a green field, in the sun. (The Armchair Book of Baseball, edited by John Thorn, (New York: Charles Scribner's Sons, 1985),(pp 141 - 143).

I had become an admirer of Giamatti and felt profoundly sad over his passing. I considered him the most erudite person associated with the game of baseball, with the possible exception of Moe Berg, the late catcher who played with the Brooklyn Dodgers, the Chicago White Sox, the Cleveland Indians, the Washington Senators and the Boston Red Sox. Thus 1989 ended on a somewhat sombre note for me: the Blue Jays' failure to capture the American League Pennant and move to the World Series; the closure of the Canadian Baseball Hall of Fame and the loss of the Commissioner of Baseball.

However, like a renewal of faith, the new year started with good news in the baseball world. On January 10, Jim Palmer and Joe Morgan were announced as the choices for enshrinement in Cooperstown, by the Baseball Writers' Association of America. Developments followed that were equally positive: the Toronto Maple Leaf Baseball Club's season - opening forum featured baseball giants Luis Tiant, Larry Doby, Denny McLain, Don Larsen, Willie Stargell and Warren Spahn; the Canadian Baseball Hall of Fame Dinner which featured Earl Weaver, Mel Allen, Chuck Tanner, Charlie Finley, Gene Mauch and Alvin Dark among the head table guests. A trip to the All - Star game in Chicago rounded out the first part of the year. Before long, it was time for my yearly pilgrimage to the baseball Mecca.

My 1990 trip to Cooperstown was not particularly eventful. I left Toronto on Saturday, August 4, accompanied by my grandson Dairl and two friends. I made a couple of tours of the Hall of Fame, one on Saturday, the second on Sunday. Torrential downpours on Sunday forced the postponement of the Induction Ceremonies to Monday. More rain on Monday caused the Ceremonies to be moved indoors to a local school where there was barely enough room to accommodate Hall of Fame members and their relatives and special invitees. Several thousand ordinary fans were unable to witness the Ceremonies. Many people were bitterly disappointed, especially those who had come for the first time to join in paying tribute to Jim Palmer and Joe Morgan only to be denied the opportunity to do so. Few understood that Hall of Fame Officials had no option but to move the proceedings indoors. It would have been unsafe to expose the Hall of Famers to the incessant downpour of rain as many of them were well advanced in age and some were ill or infirm. My friends were among the disappointed. They were first time visitors and looked forward eagerly to seeing the Hall of Famers. They were however, quite impressed by the exhibits in the Hall of Fame.

Later in the day, after we had left Cooperstown, Jim Palmer and Joe Morgan had their plaques dedicated by Commissioner "Fay" Vincent. Jerome Holtzman received the J. G. Taylor Spink Award for excellence in baseball writing and Byrum Saam was given the Ford C. Frick Award for outstanding baseball broadcasting. Twenty immortals were on hand to welcome the two "rookies" to their ranks. They were introduced in the following order according to the records of the Hall of Fame: Bob Feller, Al Barlick, Bob Lemon, Johnny Mize, "Buck" Leonard, Billy Herman, Monte Irvin, Bobby Doerr, Robin Roberts, Willie Stargell, George Kell, Billy Williams, Enos Slaughter, Willie McCovey, "Pee Wee" Reese, Stan Musial, Warren Spahn, Ted Williams, Charlie Gehringer and Ralph Kiner.

As we drove home in the rain and fog, I reflected on the weekend as a totality. Although many events of the weekend were rained out, including the Hall of Fame game, I still considered the trip worthwhile. It has always been a thrill for me to walk through the hallowed chambers of the Hall of Fame and I enjoyed doing so on this occasion as much as I did at other times. I had the chance to visit old friends and make new ones. And the other members of my group enjoyed their tour of the Hall, which was the main reason for their visit.

STAN "THE MAN" MUSIAL TAKES A SWING IN ACKNOWLEDGING FANS' APPLAUSE ON INDUCTION DAY.

I returned home and received the shocking news of the death of my friend Joe Rutkowski of Hamburg, New York. He and his wife Dena had been visiting friends in Germany when he suffered a heart attack. Joe was in his early forties. I had met the Rutkowskis in the mid-eighties at a ball game at Exhibition Stadium. One of the friendliest, most gentle human beings I knew, Joe always had a smile and a kind word for everyone. As I sat in our living room reading of his death, I wept for a friend who had died so young.

September proved to be a month with a silver lining. Blue Jays pitcher Dave Stieb, who had flirted with immortality on several occasions, finally pitched a no - hitter against the Indians in Cleveland on Sunday, the 2nd. I was in Montreal's Olympic Stadium watching the Expos play the Dodgers when the news of Stieb's achievement was flashed on the scoreboard. Two weeks later, on September 17, the Blue Jays set a Major League single season attendance record with 3,635,829 fans, surpassing the previous record of 3,608,881 set by the Dodgers in 1982.

I contacted the National Baseball Hall of Fame and Museum in Cooperstown and offered to donate a few items to commemorate the record; my offer was accepted and I sent an unused ticket, a clear celluloid ticket holder, a copy of the Blue Jays Programme/Scorebook and my scoresheets for the game. The Hall of Fame mailed an agreement form for me to sign, granting them full rights to the articles. Assuming that the Blue Jays had taken the initiative to have the record registered with the Hall of Fame, and assuming as well that I was employed by the Blue Jays, Hall officials sent the agreement form to the Blue Jays. After waiting for fifteen months without hearing anything further on the matter, I enquired and learned of the unfortunate mix-up. As fall grew into winter, my trials and tribulations continued. My father became ill and passed away in Guyana on October 22. He had been sick earlier in the year and I planned to visit him and my mother in December. His relapse made me move my visit forward; I spent a week with my parents. Two days after I returned to Canada my father died. He was seventy-seven years old; I started writing this book on December 11, 1990.

The new year started with a mixture of negative and positive developments: "Old Aches and Pains", Hall of Famer Luke Appling died at age eighty-three. On January 8, the results of the Baseball Writers' Association of America balloting were announced: Rod Carew, Gaylord Perry and Ferguson Jenkins were chosen to enter the baseball Shrine. Fergie's election was an historic moment for baseball and for Canada, as he became the first Canadian to receive baseball's ultimate honour.

There was doubt in some quarters as to whether Fergie was indeed the first Canadian to enter the Hall of Fame. In 1946, a Hall of Fame committee that had been established earlier by Commissioner Landis, (he died in 1944), initiated the Honour Rolls of Baseball. Chosen for this distinction were five managers, eleven executives, eleven umpires and twelve writers. Among the umpires was Canadian Bob Emslie, hence the belief by some that he was the first Canadian to enter the Hall of Fame. Selection to the Honour Rolls however, did not confer automatic membership in the more august body, the Hall of Fame. This is clearly evident by the fact that quite apart from the members of the Honour Rolls, eleven players were named to the Hall of Fame by the committee in the same year. Furthermore, no addition has ever been made to the Honour Rolls and six of its members considered worthy of elevation to the Hall of Fame, were subsequently duly accorded their place therein. Ed Barrow, Tom Connolly and Bill Klem were inducted in 1953; Miller Huggins and John Montgomery Ward in 1964 and Billy Evans in 1973. Fergie Jenkins can, therefore, rightly lay claim as the first Canadian entrant into baseball's Pantheon.

In late February, the Veterans' Committee announced that Bill Veeck and Tony Lazzeri were its nominees for residence in the Shrine. In the wake of the two sets of selections for baseball immortality, I received word that Ken Smith had passed away and was buried in Lakewood Cemetery overlooking James Fenimore Cooper's Lake Glimmerglass. It was reported that the Hall of Fame had purchased the plot in Lakewood Cemetery hoping to have Casey Stengel buried there. Casey's body was, however, interred elsewhere. Smith and former umpire Emmett Ashford are the only residents on the Hall of Fame's plot in Lakewood. A week later, James "Cool Papa" Bell was also called to play ball in the Big League in the sky.

A series of exciting and wonderful events followed as yet again, a renewal began. A week in Florida for Spring Training was followed by a visit from baseball royalty, as the Yankee Clipper, Joe DiMaggio, was the guest of honour at the Canadian Baseball Hall of Fame Fund-raising Dinner. Also featured were such luminaries as Bob Feller, Bobby Doerr, Fergie Jenkins, Johnny VanderMeer and Ken Keltner, the man whose sparkling play at third base for the Indians on July 17, 1941 prevented DiMaggio from extending his fifty-six consecutive games hitting streak.

On the heels of the DiMaggio visit came the Baseball Maple Leaf Forum. Fergie returned for the occasion and was joined by Johnny Mize, Warren Spahn, Denny McLain and Bert Campaneris. In May, I made a quick trip to Cooperstown to verify information and conduct additional research for my book and, in early June, I visited Memorial Stadium for a weekend series between the Blue Jays and the Baltimore Orioles, as the guest of two of my fellow Cooperstown pilgrims. While attending one of the games, I made friends with Tom and Joyce Harmes whose son Kris was a catcher in the Blue Jays organization. And on June 22, one of the happiest events of my life occurred. On that day, baseball took a back seat to the marriage of my daughter Sharon - the fourth of my five children. A happy event indeed to bring the first half of the year to a joyous climax.

The sixty-second All-Star game was played in Toronto's Skydome on Tuesday, 9th July, the first time that the Blue Jays hosted the mid - summer showpiece. The festive atmosphere that surrounds the All-Star game was more pronounced than ever before. Featured events included "Fanfest", a week long festival for fans in which tens of thousands of people were able to view scores of exhibits, test their skills in contests, obtain autographs of players, sample ball park foods and receive baseball related souvenirs from many of the participating exhibitors. Blue Jays Fan Club members assisted in several of the scheduled events, from welcoming players at the airport to serving as bartenders at parties. I obtained tickets for all the members of my family to watch the All - Star game which was won by the American League 4 - 2.

It was now time for my most important baseball undertaking of the season: my pilgrimage to Cooperstown, a pilgrimage that turned out to be the most satisfying of all. A couple of months earlier, I had been asked by the Canadian Baseball Hall of Fame to organize a busload of fans in support of our countryman Fergie Jenkins at the Induction Ceremonies. I decided to travel ahead of the bus group in order to ensure that all the bases were covered for a successful trip. On Thursday, July 18, I spent the evening watching the Blue Jays beat the Texas Rangers 4 - 0 at the Skydome. After about two hours rest, I left early in the morning of Friday the 19th for Utica en route to Cooperstown, accompanied by my grandson Dairl.

Accommodations had been arranged at the Howard Johnson Lodge. My grandson and I checked in and continued on our journey to Cooperstown, arriving around 11:15 am. I picked up literature from the Chamber of Commerce office, took gift packages to my Cooperstown friends and made a quick trip to the Hall of Fame to collect a list of the Hall of Famers who were expected to honour us with their presence during the weekend. I then set about my main task for the day, the primary reason for coming ahead of the Canadian delegation: obtaining autographs of Fergie Jenkins on forty-five T-shirts for our group. With some difficulty due, for the most part to the good security system at the Otesaga Hotel where Jenkins was staying, I was able to make contact with him. On the steps of the Otesaga, he signed the white shirts printed with a portrait of him in his Cubs uniform and a listing of some of his accomplishments on the front. My grandson assisted me with this project. I thanked Fergie for his gracious gesture, assuring him that on Induction Day the T-shirts would be worn with pride by members of our group.

I went to the Hall of Fame offices and collected complimentary passes for myself and four others. These were for admission to the Hall of Fame - I had my paid membership pass - and for entry into the special invitees area on Induction Day. Dairl and I registered for Saturday's autograph session, paid a courtesy call to Hall of Fame Librarian Tom Heitz and viewed some of the exhibits in the Hall. I had long since discovered that it was difficult to devote several hours to a single visit of the Hall, as many activities made demands on my time during an Induction weekend. Small increments of an hour or two on each level afforded me the flexibility to attend to other matters as circum-stances dictated. We spent a couple of hours with my friends, Dave and Kathy Fundis, before returning to Utica.

At the crack of dawn, amid protestations from my grandson that he did not have sufficient sleep, we drove to Cooperstown. Following breakfast at the Short Stop restaurant, we wandered along the streets for about an hour taking in the early morning sights and sounds of the Village coming to life. Vendors were laying out their displays; visitors were jockeying for parking spaces and converging on the restaurants while others were buying souvenirs. For my part, I passed the better part of an hour in the Hall of Fame Gallery in commu-nion with my heroes, focusing as I had done on previous occasions on some of the less-heralded luminaries such as Elmer Flick, Rube Marquard, Sam Rice and Ross Youngs. I left the chamber, as always, with increased enthusiasm and exuberance. After buying souvenirs from the gift shop, I rejoined Dairl and we proceeded to the A.C. Clark Gymnasium where the autograph sessions were being held.

Dairl and I were in separate lines. The rules stipulated that only flat items were to be presented for signatures. Balls, bats, and other round objects caused problems for some Hall of Famers. I took books and baseball cards and between us, we obtained an impressive collection of autographs, including those of "Yogi" Berra, Juan Marichal and Luis Aparicio. Dairl registered for the children's autograph session on Sunday before we had to hurry back to Utica to meet the busload of fans from Canada. Unfortunately, they had arrived, checked in and left for Cooperstown. I returned to the Village and joined them. Later that evening, I distributed the T-shirts that Fergie had auto-graphed.

Induction Day 1991

I woke up in fine spirits and left with Dairl just before daybreak for Cooperstown, getting to Cooper Park around 6:15 am. I sought out returning pilgrims and located many of my old friends from around Canada and the United States. We exchanged greetings and talked about baseball. As was my custom, I distributed gifts and then spent time among my Canadian col-leagues before taking my grandson to the autograph session. Among the prized signatures obtained was the "Splendid Splinter" Ted Williams' on my copy of his book, "My Turn at Bat".

Upon returning to Cooper Park, I joined friends for a while before attend-ing to my customary tasks: securing HOF cachets, Induction Day covers and programmes, and another journey through time among the exhibits in the Hall of Fame. When I returned to Cooper Park, activity was heating up. The crowd had increased considerably and would eventually exceed ten thousand. Several busloads of fans and friends of Fergie Jenkins from Chatham, Ontario, his birthplace, and from the surrounding area, came to join in saluting him. A full orchestra accompanied this group and entertained the crowd through the period leading up to the start of the Ceremonies. Around 2:15 pm, I left my friends and companions to take up my seat in the fenced-off area reserved for accredited guests. I felt somewhat guilty about abandoning my fellow pil-grims; on the other hand, I was absolutely thrilled to be accorded the honour of sitting among the distinguished guests, thanks to my work at the Canadian Baseball Hall of Fame and to Fergie. I sat next to former New York Mets and Los Angeles Dodgers first baseman Tim Harkness and his wife Barbara.

On the platform adjoining the National Baseball Library and facing Cooper Park, BBWAA President Kit Stier took to the microphone at 2:35 pm and opened the Ceremonies. George Grande made his customary introduction of the returning immortals who had come to receive the new members into their fraternity. To thunderous applause, they marched up the walkway, gestured appreciatively and took their seats. On this occasion we greeted our heroes in the following order: Early Wynn, Al Barlick, Joe Morgan, Bob Lemon, Al Lopez, Juan Marichal, Monte Irvin, "Yogi" Berra, Willie McCovey, Robin Roberts, Enos Slaughter, Bob Feller, Al Kaline, Rick Ferrell, Johnny Mize, "Pee Wee" Reese, Billy Williams, Brooks Robinson, Luis Aparicio, Bobby Doerr, "Whitey" Ford, Charlie Gehringer, Ernie Banks, Ted Williams, Joe DiMaggio and Ralph Kiner.

Prayers and a silent tribute to baseball people who were called up to a Higher League, preceded the national anthems, this year from three nations, as three Americans, a Canadian and a Panamanian were being honoured. The Panamanian Anthem was played first, then the Canadian band struck up "O! Canada". The red and white ensign fluttered in the gentle mid-afternoon breeze and scores of miniature flags were proudly clutched over the hearts of Canadians in the Park. The U.S. Anthem completed the trio. After a formal welcome by Cooperstown Mayor, Harold Hollis, media awards were given out.

Joining the ranks of celebrated scribes who received the J. G. Taylor Spink Award "for meritorious contributions to baseball writing" was Phil Collier. The former president of the BBWAA worked for the San Diego Union, covering the Pacific Coast League and later, the Los Angeles Dodgers and the Angels. Collier earned fame for his scoops, among which was the retirement of Sandy Koufax.

Joe Garagiola, former major league catcher turned broadcaster, received the Ford C. Frick Award for his outstanding work in the field of baseball broadcasting. Garagiola's knowledge of the game, coupled with a quick wit and an easy-going style, earned him the respect and admiration of all baseball fans. Garagiola served as broadcaster for the St. Louis Cardinals, the New York Yankees and the Angels. He was also a mainstay on such television programmes as N.B.C.'s "Game of the Week" and the "Today" show.

The Master of Ceremonies dispensed with a few other items then deferred to Commissioner Francis "Fay" Vincent who conducted the Dedication Ceremonies. Rod Carew's plaque was first dedicated. In a nineteen-year big league career, Carew won seven batting titles and was named American League Rookie of the Year (1967), as well as A. L. Most Valuable Player (1977). Eighteen times elected to the All-Star team, Carew has a lifetime batting average of .328 in his career with the Twins and Angels.

At last the moment eagerly awaited by Canadian fans arrived: the induction of Fergie Jenkins. Commissioner Vincent listed Fergie's achievements as a pitcher for the Phillies, Cubs, Rangers and BoSox for nineteen seasons: seven seasons with twenty or more wins, (six of those seasons being consecutive), the Cy Young Award in 1971, and the Sporting News A. L. Comeback Player of the Year in 1974. Jenkins won 284 games and is the only pitcher with three thousand (or more) strikeouts (3192) and fewer than one thousand walks (997).

The next dedication was the posthumous honouring of Tony Lazzeri who died in 1946. Lazzeri spent fourteen seasons in the Major Leagues, twelve with the Yankees and one each with the Cubs and Dodgers. A member of the Murderers' Row Yankees of 1927, arguably the greatest team ever, Lazzeri was a solid, reliable player throughout his career but playing in the shadows of the larger-than-life Babe Ruth and the "Iron Horse", Lou Gehrig, his contribution went virtually unnoticed. A lifetime .292 hitter, Lazzeri holds the A. L. single game record for runs batted-in with eleven. His widow Maye accepted his plaque.

Gaylord Perry was next to receive his plaque. With a record of 314 victories, Perry is the only pitcher to have won a Cy Young Award in each of the Major Leagues - N.L. in 1978 and A.L. in 1972. Perry saw duty with eight big league teams in a career that spanned twenty-two years. He was widely regarded as a practitioner of the spitball.

Finally, the Commissioner dedicated the plaque of Bill Veeck. As a builder, innovator and showman, Bill Veeck was in a league by himself. Deeply concerned about the fans, Veeck strove to ensure that the best possible product was put on the field for their entertainment. He signed the first black in the

American League - Larry Doby for the Indians in July 1947 - and would have up-staged Branch Rickey and the Dodgers were it not for Commissioner Landis' intervention. Veeck wanted to purchase the Phillies in 1943 and place blacks on the roster but Judge Landis, a staunch opponent of integration, learned of Veeck's intention and prevailed upon the Phillies' owner to find another buyer. Among Veeck's noteworthy undertakings were the installation of the exploding scoreboard in Comiskey Park, planting the ivy vines along the wall in Wrigley Field, the rendering of "Take Me Out to the Ball Game" by Harry Caray, and possibly his most famous gimmick of all: sending 3 foot 7 inch Eddie Gaedel to pinch hit against the Detroit Tigers in 1951. Bill Veeck was sometimes irreverent, sometimes iconoclastic in his approach to certain aspects of the National Pastime but he always had the best interest of the game and the fans at heart. Veeck died in 1986 and his plaque was given to his widow Mary Frances Veeck.

The five recipients in turn made acceptance speeches, each unique in tone and substance. Rod Carew was up-beat and eloquent, showering praise on several people who aided him along the way. When he mentioned the deceased, fiery Billy Martin, a peal of thunder punctuated his remarks. Carew looked skyward and stated that Billy was acknowledging him. Fergie Jenkins' reply was heart rending as he thanked those who influenced his career, in particular his wife and his mother. Fergie was so overcome by emotion when he spoke of his mother, that he had to pause for a while to compose himself. Then, still bursting with emotion, he dedicated his plaque to his eighty-four year old father, who was seated among the guests in the reserved area. Mrs. Lazzeri thanked the baseball establishment for honouring her husband, speaking softly and slowly and with deep humility. Gaylord Perry was entertaining in his response, making reference to the number of teams for which he played and joking about his reputation as a practitioner of the spitball. Mrs. Veeck concluded the speeches, delivering a dynamic address in which she spoke of the credo of her late husband, of his abiding love for baseball and of his regard for the fans. She thanked the Veterans' Committee for electing her husband to the Shrine. The proceedings were then declared closed and I took leave of my fellow devotees and the members of our bus group from Canada, as my grandson and I were to spend the remainder of the day and Monday with friends.

Monday, 22nd July - Hall of Fame Game Day.

I visited the Adsits, shopped for more souvenirs, then watched the game between the Twins and the Giants, the Twins winning 5-4. Around 4:15, joined by Dairl and my friends, I set out for home. Rain and overcast skies plagued us for most of our return journey, but my spirits were far from dampened or depressed. On the contrary, the events of the weekend left me in an exhilarant mood. I felt indescribable joy and satisfaction as I had seen some of the immortals for the first time: Luis Aparicio, Juan Marichal and "Whitey" Ford. And I had witnessed the induction of my compatriot Fergie Jenkins. In the afterglow of my pilgrimage, I felt like John Kinsella[1] when, in the movie *Field of Dreams*, he asked, "Is this heaven?" My answer was a paraphrase of the reply: "It's Cooperstown." The love affair with Cooperstown continued.

---

1.   *In the movie, Field of Dreams, John Kinsella comes back to life and plays catch with his son Ray. As he is about to leave, John asks his son, "Is this heaven?" and Ray replies, "It's Iowa."*

CHAPTER X

THE TERRIFIC TURNOUT — AUGUST 1991 TO AUGUST 1992

My high spirits carried over from Cooperstown to the Toronto Blue Jays pennant drive. The team emerged as the 1991 American League Eastern Division Champions. Unfortunately, Toronto failed for the third time to capture the League Championship, losing to Minnesota, four games to one.

The new year (1992), ushered in good news. On January 7, the Hall of Fame announced the results of the balloting by members of the Baseball Writers' Association of America. Tom Seaver and Rollie Fingers had been selected for enshrinement in the National Baseball Hall of Fame. Joining them were Hal Newhouser and Bill McGowan, named later by the Committee on Baseball Veterans.

A major booster of the Hall of Fame was lost when Jean Yawkey died in February at age eighty-three. An owner of the Boston Red Sox, Mrs. Yawkey, like her husband Tom who died in 1976, made significant contributions to the Hall of Fame. She was a major donor to the fund for the Fetzer-Yawkey building which is part of the Hall of Fame and Museum complex and was, at the time of her death, a member of the Board of Directors of the Hall of Fame.

The Toronto Blue Jays gave no indication that they would be World Series contenders, let alone be at the pinnacle of the baseball world at the end of the 1992 season, when I watched them during a week of Spring Training in March. The Jays' dismal Spring Training record of 13 wins and 18 losses was, however, quickly forgotten when they returned to Canada. They played like a team possessed, hovering around first place in their Division, taking over the lead on June 20, a spot they were to occupy until the end of the season. They defeated Oakland in the ALCS and Atlanta in the World Series, becoming the first World Champions outside the U.S.A.

As a prelude to my annual trip to Cooperstown, I visited with Hall of Famers Bob Lemon and Willie Stargell who participated in opening ceremonies at the start of the season for a local Toronto baseball team. Three other baseball heroes of yesteryear — Bobby Thomson, Bill Mazeroski, and Sparky Lyle — also attended the ceremonies.

Just before daybreak on Friday, July 31, my now regular Cooperstown companion, Dairl, and I along with three friends — all first-time visitors — left in rain and fog for our pilgrimage to the baseball Shrine. Despite the depressing weather, I was in high spirits: I was, after all, going to my Mecca. Another group of first-time pilgrims whom I had persuaded to make the visit, joined us later. I spent the rest of Friday and all of Saturday orienting the newcomers, renewing friendships, obtaining autographs and souvenirs, and, of course, paying homage to my heroes in the Hall of Fame.

Induction Day
Sunday, August 2, 1992

Dawn found us en route to Cooperstown from the village of Mohawk, where we were staying for the weekend. We settled on the spacious grounds of the Alfred Corning Clark Gymnasium to await the start of the ceremonies. The hours flew by quickly as I chatted with fellow pilgrims and performed other Induction Day rituals. For the second year, I was privileged to sit in the reserved section, as friends from San Diego asked me to join them. I did so with some reluctance, for although I considered it an honour, I felt more at ease with the "regulars" — pilgrims with whom I had been sharing space over the years.

When George Grande took to the rostrum, it was to a crowd of over ten thousand Hall of Fame faithful that he introduced the largest congregation of enshrinees ever to have graced the event with their presence. Thirty-three Hall of Famers — "The Terrific Turnout" — came to welcome Tom "Terrific" Seaver and the three other inductees into their ranks. As the baseball gods came up to the platform, they were greeted with deafening outbursts of applause. These living legends of the game acknowledged their worshippers and took their seats. On this occasion, these immortals attended: "Red" Schoendienst, Al Barlick, Rick Ferrell, Luis Aparicio, Bob Lemon, Gaylord Perry, Juan Marichal, Buck Leonard, Jim Palmer, Warren Spahn, Johnny Bench, Joe Morgan, Bobby Doerr, Fergie Jenkins, George Kell, Enos Slaughter, Johnny Mize, Robin Roberts, Pee Wee Reese, Yogi Berra, Al Lopez, Al Kaline, Early Wynn, Billy Herman, Ray Dandridge, Brooks Robinson, Stan Musial, Charlie Gehringer, Billy Williams, Ted Williams, Bob Gibson, Bob Feller, and Ralph Kiner.

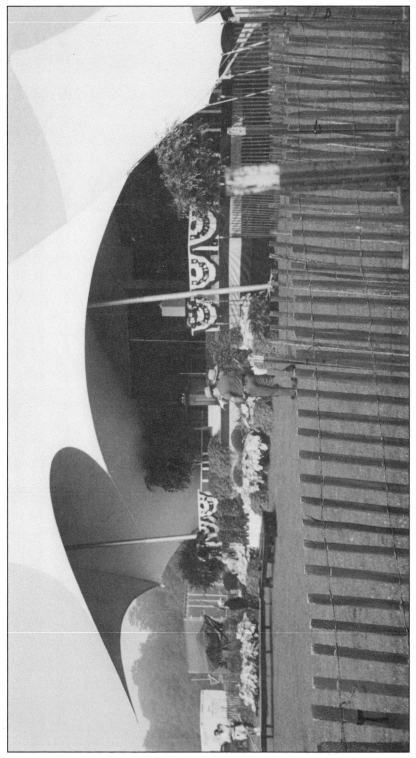

THE PLATFORM FROM WHICH THE INDUCTION CEREMONIES ARE CONDUCTED, ON THE LAWNS OF THE ALFRED CORNING CLARK GYMNASIUM. IN THE FORE-GROUND IS THE PICKET FENCE WHICH SEPARATES INVITED GUESTS FROM THE REST OF THE FANS. CHAIRS ARE PLACED IN THE FENCED-OFF AREA FOR SEATING THE INVITEES.

Other items were dispensed with, then awards were presented to members of the media. Ritter Collett received the 1991[1] J. G. Taylor Spink Award for excellence in baseball writing. Collett covered the Cincinnati Reds for the Dayton Journal and the Dayton Daily News, and is the second recipient of the Award from a city without a major league baseball team, the other being another Dayton Daily News journalist, Si Burick.

Receiving the Ford C. Frick Award for meritorious service as a baseball broadcaster, was Milo Hamilton. He gained experience with the Armed Forces Radio Network towards the end of World War II, and has since broadcast games for seven major league teams: Chicago Cubs, Chicago White Sox, St. Louis Browns, St. Louis Cardinals, Atlanta Braves, Pittsburgh Pirates, and Houston Astros whose games he still calls.

Commissioner "Fay" Vincent then dedicated the plaques of the four new entrants to the Hall of Fame. First up was Rollie Fingers whose career in the Major Leagues spanned seventeen seasons. Fingers was a relief specialist who recorded 341 regular season saves and 114 wins with the Oakland Athletics (including their dominant years in the 1970's), the San Diego Padres, and the Milwaukee Brewers. Fingers' honours include a Cy Young award (1981), the American League MVP (1981), and Fireman of the Year in both Major Leagues. He was known not only as the premier reliever of his era, but also as the proud owner of a distinctive handlebar moustache reminiscent of the style at the turn of the century. His acceptance speech reflected a deep sense of pride for his accomplishments, and for the importance of the role of the reliever.

Bill McGowan's plaque was dedicated next. Known for his durability, he was the "Iron Horse" of umpires. McGowan never missed an inning in 2,451 major league games over 16 1/2 seasons.

It was the quality of his work, however, that earned McGowan a place in baseball's Pantheon. Regarded as the finest umpire in the American League, he was respectfully nicknamed "Number 1". This esteem was reflected in the owners' unanimous decision to double his annual pension from $3,000 to $6,000 in 1954. Unfortunately, McGowan died of a heart attack two days after the increase was approved. His plaque was received by his son, Bill McGowan

---

1.   *The award is given out in the year following selection.*

Jr., who thanked the baseball establishment for bestowing the game's ultimate honour upon his father.

The Veterans' Committee corrected an injustice that had existed for over three decades when it named Hal Newhouser to the Hall of Fame. With a 207-150 won/loss record (a .580 winning percentage), four 20-victory seasons, the only major league pitcher to win consecutive MVP awards (1944 and 1945), Newhouser certainly merited much earlier entry into the Shrine. He was unfairly labelled a "wartime" pitcher, implying that he pitched to second rate hitters while the cream of the players were in the armed forces.

Newhouser gave the lie to that claim, winning 97 games and losing only 62 from 1946 to 1950, after the war had ended and the "big name" players returned to the Major Leagues. Indeed, "Prince Hal" (as Newhouser was affectionately called), came second only to Ted Williams in the 1946 voting for league MVP. In an acceptance speech that was low-key, without rancour and barely audible, Newhouser expressed gratitude for his elevation to baseball's highest order.

> "With consummate effortlessness, his was the talent that summed up baseball tradition; . . . his was the personality intensely competitive, basically decent, with the artisan's dignity that . . . seemed to recall a cluster of virtues seemingly no longer valued."

These words which appeared in Harper's magazine in 1977, were used to describe George Thomas Seaver. The article was written by a peerless baseball fan, a Yale professor who later became the President of Yale University, and subsequently the President of the National League and ultimately Commissioner of Baseball — A. Bartlett Giamatti.

Elected in his first year of eligibility for enshrinement, the likeable Seaver polled 98.8 per cent of the votes cast by the BBWAA, the highest percentage ever received by a member of the Hall of Fame. For twenty major league seasons, "Tom Terrific" performed his artistry in the service of the New York Mets, the Cincinnati Reds, the Chicago White Sox, and the Boston Red Sox. Seaver finished his career with 311 wins and 205 losses.

Among his numerous awards and honours are Rookie of the Year (1967), National League Pitcher of the Year (1969 and 1975), and Cy Young Award winner (1969, 1973 and 1975). He also shares or holds many National League records such as the lowest earned run average (2.73) for a pitcher with 200 or more wins, and most consecutive seasons (9) with 200 or more strikeouts. In a speech filled with emotion, "Tom Terrific" spoke of his deep love and respect for the game which meant so much to him. He thanked his family and friends for their support.

The Master of Ceremonies then closed the proceedings, but many pilgrims lingered to catch a glimpse of their heroes before taking leave for home. I paid a quick visit to the Hall of Fame Gallery, then left with the others for our quarters in Mohawk.

On Monday, August 3, Dairl and other members of our group obtained more autographs from Hall of Famers before we set our sights for home. As I left my Mecca after another satisfying pilgrimage, I was caught up in a wave of wistfulness which prompted me to vow to myself "I shall return."

CHAPTER XI

THE SCRIBES

Baseball is best enjoyed at a ballpark. Rapid, relatively inexpensive transportation has made it possible for increasing numbers of people to attend ballgames. There are, however, tens of thousands of avid fans who have no access to ballparks; they rely on the media to bring baseball to them. Through the newspaper, the radio and the television, fans who cannot get to the ballpark or stadium are able to follow the game, maintain allegiance to teams and identify with their heroes. While the contemporary media play an important role in bringing baseball to fans, media coverage was even more pivotal during the early days of the game, when there were fewer teams and greater distances to travel in order to get to ballparks.

The next two chapters spotlight some of the giants in the fields of baseball writing and baseball broadcasting. Their work has been taken for granted and often ignored by fans who are more interested in the score than in the medium that delivers that score, yet many of these writers and broadcasters are as legendary as the players whose exploits they have reported. This chapter focuses on the winners of the J. G. Taylor Spink Award for writers but is also intended as a tribute to many other fine journalists who have made significant contributions in reporting and in popularizing the National Pastime.

There is a common misconception that recipients of the Spink award are members of the National Baseball Hall of Fame. Often, on the days when the awards are handed out there are reports that certain writers are being inducted into the Hall of Fame. While these media greats are "Hall of Famers" in their own right and many have, indeed, been inducted into various sports and other Halls of Fame, they do not possess membership in the National Baseball Hall of Fame in Cooperstown. There is, however, an exhibit honouring them. Located on the first floor of the Library and Archive, the exhibit is entitled, "Scribes and Mikemen."

THE J. G. TAYLOR SPINK AWARD

Named after the late publisher/editor of The Sporting News J. G. Taylor Spink - the award was initiated in 1962, and honours journalists "for meritorious contributions to baseball writing". Winners[1] receive their citation in the year following selection.

BOB ADDIE

Bob Addie was one of two 1981 selections for the Spink Award. Addie had tried his hand at several jobs - lifeguard, real estate salesman, labourer, drug-store clerk, actor - before entering the field of journalism. He also served in the Army Air Corps during World War II and rose to the rank of captain. For over forty years, Addie served as a sportswriter for the <u>Washington Times - Herald</u> and the <u>Washington Post</u>; he also wrote for <u>The Sporting News</u>. For twenty of those years he covered the Washington Senators, never missing a game in all that time. He was regarded as a fan's writer, and his circle of friends included not only players and other baseball people, but also many ordinary fans. He was one of the fastest writers to complete the story of a ball game, and frequently worked on two or three articles during the course of a game: his regular story, a column for the following day and an article for <u>The Sporting News</u>. Addie was also a recipient of a National Press Club Award.

BOB BROEG

Bob Broeg received the Spink Award in 1979. A St. Louisan, Broeg played a little sandlot baseball, but passed up an opportunity to become an umpire, choosing instead to attend the University of Missouri. Years later, in 1971, the University's School of Journalism honoured him with its gold medal award, making him the first sports writer to receive the medal.

Broeg, who started his journalistic career with the <u>Associated Press</u>, was a Marine during the Second World War and joined the <u>St. Louis Post - Dispatch</u> in 1945. In 1958, he was appointed sports editor of the paper and assistant to the editor in 1977. He had a special fondness for players from baseball's earlier era, and for several years wrote nostalgic articles on old-timers for <u>The Sporting News</u>. A close friend of the Cardinal's immortal Stan Musial, Broeg is credited with giving Musial the nickname, "The Man" in 1946. The author of fifteen books, most of them on baseball, Broeg served as President of the Baseball Writers' Association of America in 1958. At the time of this writing,

---

1.   *Recipients are listed in alphabetical order, rather than chronologically, to facilitate future reference.*

Broeg was a member of the National Baseball Hall of Fame Board of Directors and a member of the Hall of Fame Committee on Baseball Veterans.

HEYWOOD BROUN

> [He] lived a full life and leaves a noble heritage. His great gifts of heart and mind and soul were ever directed toward high purposes. Neither slander nor a calumny nor thought of personal consequences ever deterred him, once he had entered a fight in the cause of right and justice as he saw it.

This tribute was paid to Heywood Broun by President Roosevelt upon Broun's death in 1939. The winner of the 1970 J. G. Taylor Spink Award, Heywood Broun's journalistic career went beyond the limits of sports coverage. During his thirty-one years in the newspaper business, he worked in many capacities ranging from war correspondent, copy reader, drama critic, sportswriter, columnist and editor. An unorthodox writer, an individualist who pioneered freedom and independence in column writing, Broun was frequently at odds with editors and publishers for his insistence that his views be printed without alteration. As a columnist writing under the title, "It Seems to me" for the Morning World, Broun took on anyone or any subject. His column was one of the most highly regarded and widely read in newspaper history.

Broun's career as a writer began with the New York Morning Telegraph in 1910. He later moved to the Tribune where he covered the Giants, becoming a friend and chess partner of the famous Giants pitcher Christy Mathewson. During World War I, he served as the Tribune's war correspondent. Broun moved in 1921 to the Morning World, and in later years worked with the World Telegram and the New York Post.

Heywood Broun will be remembered not only as a versatile writer but as a champion of the less fortunate members of his profession. During the Great Depression, he rendered assistance to many people in the newspaper field. Among those whom he put on his personal payroll was John O'Hara who later became a successful author. In 1934, in the face of opposition from some of the more established writers, Broun founded the American Newspaper Guild to assist writers in gaining better working conditions, wages, etc. He served as the Guild's president until his death in 1939. Through the Guild, he left a lasting legacy to the members of his profession.

WARREN BROWN

Warren Brown was one of three recipients of the Spink Award in 1973. He might have been a Major League ball player but chose instead to write about the game. While a student at the University of St. Ignatius in 1914, he signed with the Sacramento club of the Pacific Coast League. Upon graduation, however, he joined the <u>San Francisco Call - Post</u>, becoming the paper's sports editor while still in his early twenties. Brown later moved to the east coast as sports editor of the <u>New York Evening Mail.</u> In 1923, he moved to Chicago to become sports editor of the <u>Herald - Examiner</u> (later <u>Chicago's American)</u> and was, for many years, a columnist for <u>Chicago's American.</u>

In Chicago, Brown became friends with former White Sox owner Bill Veeck as well as distinguished people from a variety of professions, notably Jimmy Durante, Knute Rockne and Jimmy Jones. He covered forty-five consecutive World Series, starting in 1920, as part of some fifty years of sports reporting. Brown was also an accomplished after-dinner speaker and toastmaster whose wit, humour and incisive prose earned him widespread respect from readers and colleagues alike. He also worked for the <u>Chicago Sun</u> and served as Chairman of the Veterans' Committee of the National Baseball Hall of Fame.

SI BURICK

On Opening Day in 1929, a nineteen - year old pre-med student at the University of Dayton renounced his vow to Hippocrates and transferred his allegiance to Major League baseball. For the next fifty - four years Si Burick served with distinction as sports editor of the <u>Dayton Daily News.</u> The 1982 winner of the J. G. Taylor Spink Award, Burick covered many sports - baseball, horse racing, football, and boxing, to name a few. But his true love was writing about baseball. He never missed an opening day from the first time he worked the Cincinnati Reds home opener in 1929. And from 1930 he covered every World Series except 1934 and 1977.

Si Burick obtained the autographs of the top three home run hitters on one baseball - Babe Ruth in 1948, Henry Aaron in 1974 and Sadaharu Oh in 1978. He was the first Spink Award winner to have covered Major League baseball for a newspaper that was not in a Major League city, testimony to the high regard in which he was held by his peers.

JOHN P. CARMICHAEL

Ted Williams, who received many an unfair comment from the press, once said of John P. Carmichael, "He's the home run champion of sportswriters". Bill Veeck, whose White Sox was part of Carmichael's beat said, "This guy is one of the all-time greats. He knows more athletes by name - and more athletes know him by name - than any other sportswriter in the country".

Carmichael, one of two 1974 selections for the J. G. Taylor Spink Award, began his career in 1924 as an apprentice reporter for the Milwaukee Journal. In 1932 he moved to Chicago, and became a member of the Daily News staff. From 1929 to 1972, he did not miss a World Series or Spring Training game and his spirited column, "The Barber Shop" won him several awards. A much sought-after speaker at dinners, and goodwill ambassador for the White Sox, John Carmichael's style was such that he could write a good story without giving offence to anyone. He was known for going into a town and coming out with a better interview than a local writer who was closest to the ball club.

GORDON COBBLEDICK

Gordon Cobbledick was chosen posthumously for the 1977 Spink Award. Shortly after graduating from technical school in Cleveland as a mining engineer, Cobbledick's brother informed him that the best mining engineer was earning only $175.00 per month. Cobbledick quickly changed professions, joining the Cleveland Plain Dealer as a reporter on the police beat in 1923. He later moved to sports where he ultimately became sports editor. In World War I he served as a Marine, and in World War II he reported on combat for the Plain Dealer.

Cobbledick was regarded as a journalist of unquestioned fairness. His typewriter produced what former BBWAA Secretary-Treasurer Ken Smith described as, "the basic truth, insight and wisdom, but never heavy or ponderous copy". A stickler for proper writing, he urged members of his profession to read "The Elements of Style", a text that some contemporary journalists might find useful. White Sox owner Bill Veeck called Cobbledick a writer who was "good and honest, always very fair".

RITTER COLLETT

Ritter Collett is the Editor Emeritus of the <u>Dayton Daily News</u>, and holds card number one as the longest-living member of the Baseball Writers' Association of America. He is also the 1991 recipient of the J. G. Taylor Spink Award. A native of Ohio, Collett came from a newspaper family. His father was co-publisher/editor of the <u>Scranton News</u>, and Collett was delivering newspapers at the age of eleven.

While attending Ohio University, Collett worked as a student reporter for the <u>Athens Messenger</u>. Upon graduation in 1942, he joined the U.S.Army. A transfer to the Wright-Patterson Air Force Base enabled him to write for the <u>Dayton Journal</u> on a part-time basis. In 1946, he became a full-time member of the <u>Journal</u>'s staff, and sports editor in October of that same year. The <u>Journal</u> merged with the <u>Herald</u> in 1949 and became the <u>Journal-Herald</u>. Collett survived the merger and retained his job as sports editor. In 1986, the <u>Journal-Herald</u> was absorbed by the <u>Daily News</u> with Collett still writing a column.

Collett maintained a daunting schedule. He wrote a sports column six days a week, managed the <u>Journal-Herald</u> sports department, and covered the Cincinnati Reds for most of their road trips and home games. This meant writing three articles each day. He performed this routine for nearly two decades.

Ritter Collett is more than a fine sports journalist in the Dayton area. He is active in humanitarian causes. He is co-founder of the "HUTCH AWARD". Named after Fred Hutchinson who managed the Reds from 1959 to 1964, the Award recognizes a player who exemplifies the competitive spirit and character of the late Reds manager. Collett also chairs a committee that gives an annual award in honour of the late Yankee great, Lou Gehrig.

PHIL COLLIER

Phil Collier, the choice for the 1990 Spink Award, was called "Phantom" by his colleagues. Constantly on the move, Collier was seldom found where he was supposed to be. One of his profession's most energetic workers, he covered both the Dodgers and the Angels during the 1960's, working over two hundred games a year with a seven-day work week from February to October.

Collier's newspaper career started at age thirteen when he worked as a sports statistician for the <u>Baytown Sun</u> in Texas and as a stringer for semi-pro baseball for the <u>Houston Post.</u> He served in the Armed Forces during World War II, and later, in between classes at Texas Christian University, wrote for the <u>Fort Worth Star Telegram</u>. True to his custom of being where he was least expected, he upstaged Major League baseball by moving to the West Coast five years before the Dodgers and the Giants did so. In 1953 he joined the <u>San Diego Union</u>, serving as their reporter for the Pacific Coast League. He moved to the Dodgers beat, and later also covered the Angels. When the expansion Padres started in 1969, Collier covered that team as well. In 1987 he was made the <u>Union's</u> national baseball writer. He gained widespread recognition for his scoops, among them the appointment of Leo Durocher as manager of the Chicago Cubs.

Collier held the post of President of the BBWAA, was official scorer for the Dodgers, Padres and Angels and contributed articles to <u>Sports Illustrated, Copley Press, The Sporting News</u> and <u>The Associated Press</u>.

DAN DANIEL

One of three writers honoured in 1972, Daniel M. Daniel had a long, impressive career as a sports journalist with the <u>New York World Telegram and Sun.</u> He was regarded as an authority on New York Yankees history, having covered the team from the period before Babe Ruth to well into the 1960's. He wrote under a single name "Daniel", his identical first and last names. He also regularly contributed a column for the <u>Sporting News</u> under the byline "Ask Daniel", a column that dealt with questions related to baseball.

Daniel served in several organizations associated with sports. He was Chairman of the Football Writers' Association and the Boxing Writers' Association and associate Chairman of the New York City Good Conduct Committee on Sports. In addition, he was national Chairman of the BBWAA in 1957 and Chairman of the New York Chapter of the BBWAA for five years consecutively.

JOHN DREBINGER

John Drebinger was the second of the three 1973 winners of the Spink award. He was not originally slated to be a sports writer. His father, a violinist with the New York Metropolitan Orchestra, wanted Drebinger to become a concert pianist, but an injury to his thumb derailed young Drebinger's career in music. He turned to journalism with <u>The Staten Island Advance,</u> spending eight years with that paper. He then moved to <u>The New York Times</u> as a baseball writer.

For forty years Drebinger reported on the Dodgers, the Giants and the Yankees, attending nearly six thousand games. From 1929 to 1963, Drebinger covered all two hundred and three World Series games. For several of his years as a baseball writer, Drebinger chaired the New York chapter of the BBWAA.

John Drebinger was the friend and confidant of many baseball players and managers, including Babe Ruth and Casey Stengel. Easy-going, and with an infectious laugh, he was admired by his peers. A colleague, Til Ferdenzi, said of him, "I think in his time he wrote the purest and most intelligent baseball stories in the country." <u>The Times'</u> Red Smith said, "He could give a completely accurate report of a game without making it sound like Armageddon."

CHARLES DRYDEN

Charley Dryden worked for newspapers on both the east and west coasts, and some of the major baseball cities in between. His sportswriting career lasted from the early 1890's to 1921, but his vintage years were from the late 1890's to the early teens of the 20th Century. In his heyday, Dryden was regarded as the "King of baseball writers".

Dryden was first employed in a foundry but his flair for writing led him to a job with the <u>San Francisco Examiner</u> where he reported on games in the California State League and later the Pacific Coast League. At the turn of the century, he moved to the <u>American</u> in New York, and then to the <u>New York Evening World</u>. He left New York for a stint with the <u>North American</u> in Philadelphia. In 1905 he accepted an offer from the <u>Chicago Examiner,</u> and while in the windy city he also worked for the <u>Chicago Herald Examiner</u> and the <u>Chicago Tribune</u>. He earned respect both as a reliable journalist, and for his "penetrating interpretation" of the game. A founding member of the BBWAA, Dryden was chosen as the 1965 recipient of the J. G. Taylor Spink Award.

The name Charley Dryden will not ring a bell with the overwhelming majority of today's fans and indeed, many present day sports writers. But he left all of baseball a lasting legacy — his humour and witticisms. It was Dryden, for example, who referred to the Washington Senators as "Washington - first in war, first in peace and last in the American League". And it was Dryden who dubbed Frank Chance (of Tinker to Evers to Chance fame), "The Peerless Leader", and who christened the 1906 White Sox, "The Hitless Wonders", an epithet by which they are still remembered to-day. These terms and many more form Dryden's lasting contribution to the lore and terminology of baseball.

HUGH FULLERTON

Hugh Fullerton was accorded the honour of being chosen winner of the 1964 Spink award. Fullerton is perhaps best known for "Fullerton's Folly", a seemingly ludicrous prediction that the team Dryden dubbed "The Hitless Wonders" would in fact go on to win the 1906 World Series. After all, a team with a .230 batting average and 93 wins (the White Sox) beating the Cubs, a team with a batting average of .262 and 116 wins! Fullerton, however, was no fool. He had a keen, incisive mind and a penchant for breaking down statistics, analyzing them and using the information to spot winners.

Fullerton started his career with the Cincinnati Enquirer, and later moved to Chicago and worked for the Record and the Tribune; He next went to New York with the Evening World, and afterwards, the Evening Mail. In 1922 he became associate editor of Liberty magazine, re-entering mainstream reporting six years later with the Columbus Dispatch. A regular contributor to The Sporting News, Fullerton authored several books on sports, and was among the early writers who became members of the BBWAA.

At the time of the "Black Sox" affair, Fullerton was among the first to detect that something was amiss. Torn by his abiding love for baseball and his affection for the White Sox players, he nevertheless left no stone unturned in his quest for the truth. Put simply, Fullerton believed that the White Sox were just too powerful a team to lose the Series. When he first hinted that Chisox players had thrown the 1919 World Series, he became the object of scorn and ridicule from many quarters, including the media. Through his initial investigations, and later through the work of others, Fullerton's belief that something was amiss proved in the end to be right.

FRANK GRAHAM

A young man walked into the office of Ned Brown, sportswriter with the New York Daily Mail in 1911, and asked for a job. When told that they could not pay much, the young man declared that the money did not matter. Although employed at the time by the telephone company, he wanted the job with the Mail because he hoped to become a fulltime sportswriter. His enthusiasm and confidence landed him the job. His first assignment was to cover a training session of boxer Abe Attell who would later be involved in the 1919 World Series scandal. Thus began the brilliant career of Frank Graham, a career which earned him the 1971 J.G.Taylor Spink Award.

Graham, after free-lancing with Boxing Magazine, the New York Morning World, and the New York Evening Sun, joined the Sun full time in 1915. He eventually succeeded the respected Joe Vila as editor of the sports column "Setting the Sun", a post he occupied from 1934 to 1943. He also worked for Look magazine and the Journal - American. Graham rarely criticized the athletes about whom he wrote. It was said that "his style enabled readers of his column to hear and see what occurred where their tickets did not allow them to go — the locker room, the manager's quarters and the club house. He wrote several books on sports, including, The New York Yankees, The New York Giants, The Brooklyn Dodgers and Lou Gehrig: A Quiet Hero.

TOMMY HOLMES

During the 1948 World Series Boston Braves owner Lou Perini held a party at the Somerset Hotel. One of the guests was Tommy Holmes, the writer. Another guest was Tommy Holmes, the baseball player for the then Boston Braves. Writer Holmes could not attend the function, so he telephoned the Hotel to inform Perini. As soon as he announced his name, the voice at the other end of the telephone said, "Oh, no, you're not. Tommy Holmes is standing right where I can see him". This confusion between Tommy Holmes the baseball writer and Tommy Holmes the baseball player often resulted in numerous misdirected telegrams, telephone calls and letters over the years when they were both active in their respective occupations. There was, however, no confusion regarding the superb writing of Tommy Holmes the reporter. For his work, he was honoured by his peers in 1979 with the J. G. Taylor Spink Award.

Holmes was considered a keen student of baseball. He read widely, and exuded a warmth that endeared him to his associates. A die-hard fan of the Brooklyn Dodgers, Holmes nevertheless was still able to write objectively about the team. He started with the Brooklyn Eagle, moving to the New York Herald Tribune thirty years later when the Eagle ceased operations. In 1947 Holmes served as President of the BBWAA. When he died in 1971 Red Smith of the New York Times said Tommy Holmes was "the best baseball writer of his time, possibly the best ever".

JEROME HOLTZMAN

Jerome Holtzman is often referred to as a baseball scholar, and this is evident in his work. In 1989 he was singled out for the J. G. Taylor Spink Award. A baseball writer for over forty years, Holtzman's list of accomplishments includes the invention of the "save" rule for relief pitchers, and a highly acclaimed book, "No Cheering in the Press Box".

In the early 1940's, fresh from high school, Jerome Holtzman went to work for the Chicago Daily Times where he started as a copy boy. He served in the Marines for two years, then returned to writing. After the War Holtzman was associated with both the Chicago Sun - Times and the Chicago Tribune. He continues to write for the Chicago Tribune. A regular contributor to The Sporting News, his articles have appeared in Baseball Digest, Saturday Evening Post, Sports Illustrated and Sport magazine. As a youngster whose heroes were sports writers, Jerome Holtzman grew up to become a sportswriter himself, emerging as one of the best in his field.

BOB HUNTER

He sold his law books for thirteen dollars, quit law school and took a job for six dollars a week with the Los Angeles Post - Record. The year was 1932 and Bob Hunter was within one semester of graduating from Southwestern Law School. For over fifty years thereafter, Hunter worked in the newspaper business.

In 1933 Bob Hunter moved to the L.A.Examiner (later the Herald - Examiner following the merger of the Examiner and the Herald - Express). He has reported on the Padres, the Angels and the Dodgers, and wrote a column,

"Bobbin' Around". He is best described as sharp and hard hitting, a stubborn and resourceful journalist who left no stone unturned in his efforts to get to the bottom of a story. His credits include writing the script of the T.V. series, "Double Play with Durocher Day", (featuring Leo "The Lip" Durocher and actress wife Laraine Day). He was official scorer for several All - Star and World Series games, Chairman of the Los Angeles branch of the BBWAA, and national Chairman of the BBWAA. In 1988 he was one of two selections for the Spink Award.

JAMES ISAMINGER

The second of the 1974 winners of the J. G. Taylor Spink Award, James Isaminger, began his journalistic career with the <u>Cincinnati Times - Star</u>. He moved to the <u>Philadelphia North American</u> in 1905 upon the recommendation of a former Cincinnati sportswriter, Byron Bancroft Johnson, who was then President of the American League. When the <u>North American</u> went out of operation, Isaminger joined the <u>Inquirer</u>. He had a flair for statistics and was first editor, and then co-author, of the annual baseball guides produced by Reach and later by Spalding.

Isaminger served as President of the BBWAA in 1935. During the Black Sox scandal in 1919, his investigative work was surpassed only by Hugh Fullerton's in getting to the truth of the affair.

HAROLD KAESE

Harold Kaese was the 1976 recipient of the Spink Award. Before he entered the world of sports writing, Kaese was an outstanding school athlete participating in basketball, baseball, track and field, sailing and squash. At one point, he was captain of the track and field, baseball and basketball teams. Kaese graduated with an honours degree in English in 1933 and his facility with the English language was reflected in his pinpoint grammatical accuracy. A statistician and an historian as well, he possessed more than a working knowledge of several sports, but he focused mainly on baseball. He was the repository of a wealth of information on baseball. He also carried a little black book which he consulted for answers to trivia questions.

Kaese joined the <u>Boston Globe</u> in 1948 and later had his own column until his retirement in 1973. One of his greatest admirers was Moe Berg, the scholarly baseball catcher of the Red Sox.

RAY KELLY

Despite a seventh-grade education, this second winner of the 1988 J. G. Taylor Spink Award excelled in his profession and rose to a position of prominence shared by only a select few. An abiding love of sports and a flair for reporting enabled him to overcome his lack of formal education and achieve such heights.

At fifteen, Ray Kelly was a copy boy, running errands and delivering proofs for the <u>Philadelphia Evening and Sun Bulletin.</u> He moved up to reporting on minor events in Philadelphia and the surrounding area. After serving in the US Army during World War II, he began covering the Philadelphia Athletics, and took on the Phillies beat in 1955 when the Athletics left for Kansas City. Kelly worked for several local papers up to his death in 1988. He held the post of President of the BBWAA and also served as President of the Philadelphia branch. Ray Kelly was an excellent soccer player. On one occasion, he played in a championship game and scored the winning goal. However, he had been assigned by his newspaper to cover the match. His bosses did not know that he played in the game as well so Kelly reported that someone else had scored the winning goal.

JOHN KIERAN

Officials at Yale University created a furore when they invited a sportswriter to give the keynote address at one of their functions. How could an institution of higher learning lower its standards by asking a baseball writer to speak? Criticism flew from many quarters. Undaunted, the sportswriter delivered his speech as planned, and embarrassed his detractors by giving the address in perfect Latin. That writer, John Kieran, was the third 1973 selection for the J. G. Taylor Spink Award.

Kieran was not only a fine sportswriter, he was also a standout in many other fields. A naturalist specializing in bird life, an historian, and a scholar of the classics, Kieran also had more than a passing interest in art, classical music, chemistry and astronomy. Kieran was a walking encyclopedia. Regarded in his day as the dean of quiz experts, he gained national prominence as a panellist on the hit radio programme "Information Please", answering questions on every conceivable subject. "Information Please" dominated the radio waves from 1938 to 1948, and John Kieran was its star performer.

After graduating with honours from Fordham University in 1912, Kieran spent some time working at various jobs: teacher, office boy, foreman, time-keeper and assistant superintendent for a sewer project. In 1915, he began writing for the New York Times reporting on baseball, golf, swimming and tennis. At the time of the Mexican Border Campaign, he was given the responsibility of covering a detachment of the New York National Guard.

Kieran enlisted with a New York volunteer unit — the 11th Engineers — during the First World War. He served in France and returned as a second lieutenant. After the war, he wrote on sports for the New York Tribune and the New York Herald. In 1927 he rejoined the Times with a column entitled, "Sports of the Times", becoming the first person to have a signed column in that newspaper. Kieran crossed over to the New York Sun as a syndicated columnist in 1943 and retired from the newspaper business in 1945.

LEONARD KOPPETT

This co-winner of the 1992 J. G. Taylor Spink Award moved to the United States from Russia at the age of five, and grew up to become one of the outstanding sportswriters of his era. Leonard Koppett is regarded as the mentor of many writers, an intellectual, and an original thinker.

Koppett spent his childhood and youth in the New York area — Brooklyn, Manhattan and the Bronx, making him eminently qualified to write about the New York ball clubs. In fact, from the late 1940's to the early 1970's, he covered all of the New York teams. Koppett served in the U.S. Army from 1943 to 1945. He returned to New York in 1945, and completed his studies at Columbia University in 1946. While at Columbia, he held several media-related positions at the same time. He wrote for the university newspaper, assisted in running the publicity department and the radio station, and served as campus correspondent for the New York Times, the Herald-Tribune, and the Associated Press.

In 1947, Koppett became a full-time writer for the Herald-Tribune. He moved to the Post in 1954, and then to the Times in 1963. He covered the Dodgers, the Giants, and the Yankees. He went to the west coast in 1973 as the Times correspondent, but resigned in 1978 to work for the Peninsula Times-Herald. Koppett also wrote a column for the Sporting News for seventeen years.

But Koppett is more than an erudite sportswriter. He is a man for all seasons. He has written several books, among them <u>The New Thinking Fan's Guide to Baseball</u>, and <u>The Man in the Dugout</u>. Koppett is currently planning to write his tenth book, a work on the history of baseball. He has held positions in the Football, the Basketball and the Baseball Writers' Associations. A patron of the arts, Koppett is an expert on the theatre, music, opera and all kinds of statistics. Joseph Durso of the <u>New York Times</u> called Koppett "the Cicero of the Press Box".

JACK LANG

In 1986, Jack Lang was chosen as the recipient of the Spink Award, forty years after he started covering the Brooklyn Dodgers for the <u>Long Island Press</u>. During that span, he served his profession with distinction as a dedicated, hard working journalist, rising to prominence as Chairman of the New York chapter of the BBWAA and national Secretary-Treasurer of the Association.

Following the Dodgers' move to Los Angeles, Lang worked the Yankees beat in the heyday of the Mantle-Ford era. He returned to covering the National League when the Mets emerged in 1962. He wrote for the <u>Long Island Press</u> until it ceased publication in 1977. He was then hired for the Mets beat by the <u>New York Daily News</u>.

When Lang, as Secretary-Treasurer of the BBWAA, called former Cardinal Joe Medwick in 1968 to inform Medwick that he had been elected to the Hall of Fame, it was Lang's second call to "Ducky" Medwick. Thirty-four years earlier, in 1934, a thirteen year old Jack Lang had pursued Medwick for an autograph which he obtained after considerable perseverance. The author of a number of books, including "<u>The New York Mets - Twenty-five years of Baseball Magic</u>", Lang has been a correspondent for <u>The Sporting News</u> for over twenty years.

RING LARDNER

He was a tall man — taller than most baseball writers of his day — and it was said that "Ring" Lardner also towered above others in his genius for writing and for expressing his thoughts. His contemporaries such as Grantland

Rice, Hugh Fullerton and Damon Runyon — held him in high regard. His profession recognized his brilliance and made him the first selection (in 1963) for the J. G. Taylor Spink Award, after Spink himself was cited for the honour in 1962.

Ringgold Wilmer Lardner played baseball in high school. He started writing about baseball in Boston and St. Louis. Most of his work, however, was done in Chicago where he covered the Cubs during the era of Tinker, Evers, Chance and "Three - finger" Brown. He later covered the White Sox beat where he developed a close friendship with the Sox manager, "Kid" Gleason. Lardner was profoundly affected by the "Black Sox" scandal in 1919 and lost some of his feeling for the game as a result. He collaborated with Hugh Fullerton in getting to the facts of the scandal. After Ed Cicotte, the ace pitcher of the White Sox lost a game 9 - 1, Lardner painfully remarked, "I don't like what these owl eyes of mine have been looking at. I think I smell something and its smells like rotten fish." Later, when the facts of the scandal had been revealed, Lardner, to the tune of "I'm Forever Blowing Bubbles," satirically sang, "I'm forever throwing ball games, pretty ball games in the air".

In Chicago he had a column in the <u>Tribune</u> and became a much sought after contributor to many of the nation's top publications. As editor of the <u>Sporting News</u> from 1910 to 1911, his column "Pullman Pastimes" led him to write a <u>Saturday Evening Post</u> series, "You Know Me Al", which featured humorous stories about baseball players of the period 1910 to 1920. Grantland Rice thought that "Ring" was "A fine baseball writer", the closest to being a genius of anyone he knew. Regarded as one of the finest short - story writers in the country, Ring Lardner has earned a place in American literature achieved by no other baseball writer, with the possible exception of Damon Runyon.

EARL LAWSON

When Earl Lawson retired as baseball writer for the <u>Cincinnati Post and Times - Star</u> in 1985, he ended a thirty - four year career that saw him move up from a lowly copy boy to become one of the most highly acclaimed members of his fraternity. In his teens, Lawson started as a copy boy for the <u>Cincinnati Times - Star</u>. Two years later, while still in his teens, he became a member of the reporting staff. After a three - year break for service in World War II he returned to the <u>Times - Star</u> and was assigned to sports, taking over the Reds beat in 1951. When the paper went out of business in 1958, Lawson shifted to the <u>Cincinnati Post and Times - Star,</u> where he maintained coverage of the Reds until his retirement. In 1985, he was chosen to receive the J. G. Taylor Spink Award.

Lawson continued to write on a limited basis after 1985, penning a weekly column for the <u>Post and Times - Star.</u> He developed strong friendships with many players and other Reds personnel during his long tenure as a reporter. Regarded as the dean of Cincinnati sportswriters, Earl Lawson served as President of the BBWAA in 1977. Of his work he once said, "It's a fun job. Not too many people get paid to go see ball games."

ALLEN LEWIS

Allen Lewis, who joined Bob Addie as the other 1981 selection for the J. G. Taylor Spink Award, spent three decades on the Philadelphia Phillies beat. From 1949 to his retirement in 1979, Lewis worked for the <u>Philadelphia Inquirer.</u> When he started, reporting was confined to what occurred on the field between the white lines. Later, when coverage was extended to include post - game analysis, quotes from players and so on, he made the transition easily. During his tenure on the Phillies beat, he witnessed eight managerial changes for the club.

Lewis possessed a deep understanding of baseball and was an authority on the rules of the game, so much so that he chaired the Scoring Rules Committee for twelve years. Many of the rules that are in current usage were recommended by him. Allen Lewis has also served as a member of the Hall of Fame Veterans' Committee.

FRED LIEB

The man who gave Yankee Stadium the name "The House that Ruth Built", Fred Lieb at one time held the lowest - numbered membership card in the Baseball Writers' Association of America: a card issued in 1911, the year he covered his first baseball game. Lieb was the second of three distinguished journalists to be awarded the J. G. Taylor Spink Citation in 1972.

Lieb started with the <u>New York Press</u> in 1911 and later wrote for many other newspapers, including the <u>New York Post</u>, the <u>New York Morning Sun</u>

and the <u>New York Telegraph</u>. Regarded as the top baseball historian of his time, Lieb was also one of the most widely - known sports writers. Among the scribes with whom he shared press box duties were such legends as Damon Runyon, "Ring" Lardner, Grantland Rice and Heywood Broun. His friends among legendary players included Lou Gehrig, Babe Ruth and Ty Cobb.

Fred Lieb's love for the National Pastime was developed and nurtured as a youngster in his native Philadelphia in the bleachers of the Baker Bowl and Columbia Park. After graduating from high school, he joined the <u>Philadelphia News Bureau</u>. He later spent six years with the <u>Norfolk and Western Railroad</u> and wrote a series of biographies for <u>Baseball Magazine.</u> Lieb once urged Ty Cobb to buy the Philadelphia Phillies for $300,000, an offer that the "Georgia Peach" declined.

JOE McGUFF

When Joseph McGuff was chosen for the J. G. Taylor Spink Award in 1984, it was the crowning glory of a baseball writing career that dated back to 1948. He moved from the <u>Tulsa World</u> to the <u>Kansas City Star</u> and covered the minor league Kansas City Blues. When the Athletics moved from Philadelphia to Kansas City in 1955, McGuff was assigned to that beat. In 1966, he was given his own column and was elevated to the post of sports editor, an office he held for over twenty years. McGuff covered over twenty All - Star and thirty World Series games and twice was the official scorer for the World Series.

At the tender age of five, McGuff was introduced by his father, a semipro ball player, to Eddie Grimes who was playing in the Texas League for the Tulsa Oilers. Grimes became young Joe's favourite player. Another baseball player, Canadian George "Twinkletoes" Selkirk, the New York Yankee who replaced Babe Ruth in the outfield, helped in McGuff's development and understanding of baseball. McGuff was a fledgling reporter for the <u>Kansas City Star</u> while Selkirk was managing the K. C. Blues.

TOM MEANY

"Baseball is better played today, and written better, than it was in 1923. Those who sigh for the good old days are taking refuge behind rose - coloured glasses." These words were written sometime ago by a journalist who covered his first ballgame in 1923. While he remained loyal to the era of Babe Ruth, Meany adapted to the changing times and wrote about the game as he saw it, rather than as it used to be played when he first started his beat. In 1975, this highly respected scribe, Tom Meany, was co-winner of the J. G. Taylor Spink Award, a fitting tribute to a brilliant career.

After leaving school Meany worked for the Brooklyn - Manhattan subway system before joining the <u>New York Journal</u> in 1922. A year later, he moved to the <u>Brooklyn Daily Times</u>, leaving the <u>Times</u> for the <u>New York Telegram</u>, where he covered the Giants. It was during this time that Tom Meany attracted national attention. One day in 1932, while searching for a story he went to the Giants' Polo Grounds and stumbled upon the baseball scoop of the decade. It was raining and no game was played. Meany found a note on the door of the manager's office, a note that announced the resignation of the manager: the fiery, acerbic genius whose association with the Giants spanned over thirty years - "Little Napoleon", John J. McGraw.

Tom Meany worked for other publications - <u>PM,</u> the <u>New York Star</u>, the <u>Morning Telegraph</u> and <u>Collier's</u> where he became sports editor. He free-lanced for several years then changed careers from writing about baseball to promoting it. In 1958, Meany joined the Yankees as a special projects co-ordinator. When the Mets were granted a franchise, he was appointed publicity director and later, promotions director. Author of over a dozen books, Meany was a frequent after - dinner speaker and possessed a razor sharp wit to complement a fine sense of humour. As he was leaving a party on one occasion, another guest, an unbearable bore, asked him, "Can I drive you home?" "You already have", Meany quipped. Another time in 1948, after Yankees part owner Del Webb had fired Bucky Harris as manager, Webb approached Harris at a party. Someone asked what he wanted with his ex-manager. Meany answered, "He came back for the knife".

SID MERCER

When his veracity as a reporter was questioned, this 1969 J. G. Taylor Spink Award recipient sacrificed his close friendship with the New York Giants manager to preserve the integrity of his profession. Sid Mercer and manager John McGraw had been close friends for over ten years when Mercer wrote a story in which he carried McGraw's stinging criticism of National League President,

John Tener. In what became known as "the great repudiation of 1917", McGraw issued a statement denying the report, although Mercer had shown him a copy before it went to press. Indeed, McGraw encouraged him to print the story. After several hearings and acrimonious exchanges, Mercer was cleared and John McGraw was fined.

James Sidney Mercer left his home in Paxton, Illinois at age seventeen and headed for Kansas hoping to earn five dollars per day as a farm hand. When he ran out of funds in St. Louis, he took a job as a "printer's devil"[2] with the St. Louis Republic. He later returned home, continued his education then rejoined the Republic. In 1901, the twenty - one year old Mercer was assigned to the Cardinals beat. A two year stint as travelling secretary with the St. Louis Browns followed after which he joined the staff of the St. Louis Post - Dispatch. In 1907, he moved to the Evening Globe in New York and was assigned to the Highlanders (later the Yankees) spring training camp in Atlanta. A dispute with Highlanders manager Clark Griffith over his coverage of the team resulted in Mercer switching over to the Giants.

In New York, Mercer honed his skills and blossomed into one of the finest baseball writers and an authority on the game. His associates included Sam Crane, Damon Runyon and Frank Graham. Mercer left the Globe for the Evening Journal where he had a syndicated column. When he died in 1945, two months shy of his sixty - fifth birthday, Mercer was with the merged Journal - American. Mercer also covered boxing from 1923 to 1930 and was a founding member of the BBWAA and Chairman of the New York chapter in 1919. He also served as national President in 1940. A member of the original Hall of Fame Committee, Mercer was for many years toastmaster at the annual New York baseball writers' dinner.

EDGAR MUNZEL

When Edgar Munzel of the Chicago Sun - Times was named co - winner of the J. G. Taylor Spink Award for 1977, it was the high point of a career that spanned over four decades in the field of baseball writing. As a fifteen - year old, he began his climb to the top as a copy boy with the old Chicago Herald - Examiner. After two years at Northwestern University, Munzel secured a job at the Examiner's sports desk. In 1929, at the tender age of twenty - two, he began covering the White Sox and the Cubs, spending a half of a season with

---

2.   A "printer's devil" is a printer's apprentice.

each club. He has covered over eight thousand major league games and spent more time in the company of baseball players than with his family.

Munzel believed that the role of the baseball writer changed when radio and television entered the scene. By enabling fans to hear and see ballgames, the electronic media forced the writer to shift emphasis from reporting to interpreting. While the writer still reported on the essential elements of the game, stories now included more information about aspects of the "game behind the game" - behind the scenes coverage of the club house and dugout, for example. Human interest stories and interpretive material were interwoven with the results of what occurred on the playing field. Munzel made that transition successfully.

Edgar Munzel's knowledge of the game, his durability and consistency, and his good judgement earned him a spot on the Hall of Fame Veterans' Committee. Regarded at one time as the dean of American baseball writers, he was called by Bob Broeg of the St. Louis Post - Dispatch, "A Gentleman of the Press". Munzel was also a friend and confidant of many ballplayers and other baseball people. The Chicago Cubs accorded him the honour of having him throw out the first pitch to open the 1969 season.

TIM MURNANE

An obituary in the Boston Globe on February 8, 1917 ran as follows:

> a man of the utmost simplicity of character and of wonderful ideals, which survived all the experiences of a life that makes most men cynics. He saw men truly, but he idealized the game with which most of his career was bound up. He believed in baseball sincerely as a form of character and as a great factor in making Americans better men.

This tribute was paid to Tim Murnane, one of two 1978 choices for the Spink Award. In selecting Murnane, the Committee rectified an omission that had existed for over a decade, since the commencement of the Award. Tim Murnane was one of the giants of his profession and merited selection much earlier than in 1978. More important, however, is the fact that he received due recognition, albeit sixty-one years after his death.

Timothy H. Murnane was born in Naugatuck, Connecticut in 1851. In public school he played baseball and in 1869, the year the Cincinnati Reds were established as the first professional ball club, Murnane signed as a catcher with the Stratford, Connecticut club. Murnane played with minor league teams until 1873 when he became a member of the Philadelphia Athletics. He also spent time with Boston and Providence. According to contemporary reports, Murnane was an outstanding centrefielder, ending his fifteen year major league career in 1884 with a .263 batting average.

If Tim Murnane contributed as a player in the shaping of baseball in its formative years, he had an even greater impact on the game as a writer and league official. In 1888, he was hired by the <u>Boston Globe</u> as a baseball writer moving up to the position of baseball editor. He remained with the <u>Globe</u> until his death in 1917. During his tenure with the paper Murnane assiduously worked to promote the game of baseball. He was active in several baseball organizations serving as President of the New England League for twenty-four years, President of the Eastern League, first Vice - president of the National Association and member of the Arbitration Board.

Murnane was affectionately called, "The Silver King" because of his hair. Never biting in his reports, his wit and Irish brogue made him a delightful speaker at dinners. In October 1917, a benefit All - Star game was held in Murnane's honour. The American League used the proceeds of the game to erect a monument in tribute to Murnane. Inscribed on the headstone are the following words:

> In memoriam; Timothy Hayes Murnane 1851 - 1917; pioneer of baseball; champion of its integrity; gifted and fearless writer; this monument erected by the American League.

JIM MURRAY

> Baseball was built by Ruth, Gehrig, Cobb, Willie Keeler,...Walter Johnson, Willie Mays and Henry Aaron. They are American royalty... But who would they be if there were no one to tell you about them? ... if there hadn't been a Ring Lardner, Grantland Rice, Damon Runyon, Red Smith, Jimmy Cannon or Jimmy Breslin to tell you about them? ... The baseball writer is the ultimate fan. He is the surrogate for the fan.

This excerpt is from a speech by Jim Murray made on July 31, 1988, when he received the Spink Award for 1987. He made an eloquent case for the role of the writer in the development and promotion of the game of baseball.

Murray started his journalistic career as a campus correspondent for the Hartford Times while he attended Trinity College. He was on the staff of the New Haven Register for two years and the Los Angeles Examiner for four years. He served at Time magazine for eleven years then moved to Sports Illustrated, after which he became the chief sports columnist of the Los Angeles Times.

For over twenty - five years, Murray has been one of the most widely - read columnists. A fearless writer, he has on numerous occasions aroused the ire of some people by comments such as calling Birmingham, Alabama, the "gateway to the Ku Klux Klan" and stating that Detroit "should be left on the doorstep for the Salvation Army, but I don't think they can save it". Murray is also one of the most honoured writers, having been named "America's Best Sportswriter" fourteen times. He has also received the Associated Press Sports Editors Association Citation for the best column, the "Headliners Award" and the "Red Smith Award" for meritorious sports writing.

SHIRLEY POVICH

This law school graduate chose the rough life of a baseball writer rather than the comfortable surroundings of a law practice. In 1975, Shirley Povich joined Tom Meany as winner of the J. G. Taylor Spink Award. One of the most widely - known and respected members of his profession, Povich began as a copy boy with the Washington Post in 1922 while he studied law at night at Georgetown University. At age twenty, Povich was made sports editor of the paper and spent time in the Pacific during the Second World War as a correspondent covering the Marines. From 1926 up to his retirement he had a column, "This Morning" with the Post. His association with the paper lasted for over four decades.

Shirley Povich contributed articles to the Sporting News. An authority on the Washington Senators, his knowledge of baseball and his brilliance as a writer earned him a number of prestigious awards other than the Spink, including the "Headliners Award" (1947) and the "Grantland Rice Memorial Award" (1964). Povich held the post of President of the BBWAA in 1955.

JOE REICHLER

One of two writers described by former Commissioner Bowie Kuhn as "Peerless Journalists", Joseph L. Reichler won the coveted J. G. Taylor Spink Award in 1980. This native of New York joined the <u>Associated Press</u> in 1943, after he graduated from St. John's University. An intense rivalry with aggressive co-winner Milton Richman, who reported for <u>United Press International,</u> led Reichler to develop the extensive national network of personal contacts which enabled him to scoop his colleagues on big stories such as Joe DiMaggio's retirement, Joe McCarthy's signing to manage the Red Sox and the Dodgers' move from Brooklyn to Los Angeles. Through this carefully cultivated network, Reichler was the first to learn the names of the players chosen by the American League expansion teams in 1960 and the National League in 1961. So great was his reputation for obtaining scoops that former BBWAA President Ray Kelly Jr. deemed him a "fact - ferreting, trade - sniffing" specialist. On one occasion at a meeting of major league owners, Commissioner Ford Frick swore the participants to secrecy at the end of a session. One owner opined, "That's a waste of time. You know that five minutes after we leave here, Joe Reichler will know everything that took place."

Reichler served as editor of MacMillan's <u>Official Baseball Encyclopedia.</u> He was also a prolific writer, with articles in <u>Sports Illustrated,</u> <u>Sport Magazine,</u> the <u>Street and Smith Yearbook,</u> <u>Saturday Evening Post</u> and <u>Collier's</u>. Books authored by him include, *Baseball's Greatest Moments, The Game and the Glory, It's Good to Be Alive* and *The World Series*. After almost a quarter of a century with <u>Associated Press</u>, Reichler left to become Director of Public Relations in the Baseball Commissioner's office. He was later appointed Special Assistant to the Commissioner.

GRANTLAND RICE

> *"For when the One Great Scorer comes*
> *to mark against your name,*
> *He writes - not what you won or lost -*
> *but how you played The Game."*

How many times have we used these words over the years when referring to sportsmanship? These are the last two lines of the final stanza of the poem,

"Alumnus Football," written by Grantland Rice over half a century ago. The Poet Laureate of the bards of the press - box, Rice was called one of "nature's noblemen", "a patriot" and "the greatest sportswriter of his era". This gentle man whose goodwill and friendship knew no bounds, who had an award named in his honour, was singled out for the J.G. Taylor Spink Award in 1966.

Henry Grantland Rice was born in 1880. While attending Vanderbilt University, he played baseball as the regular shortstop and also played football. After graduation with honours, Rice accepted a job as sports editor of the Nashville Daily News, moving over to the Atlanta Journal in 1902. While with the Journal, he received several telegrams urging him to go see the country's most promising young ballplayer. His journalist's curiosity led Rice to Anniston, Georgia, where he got his first big story watching Tyrus Raymond Cobb play. From that day on, Rice followed the progress of the "Georgia Peach" and a lasting acquaintanceship developed between the two. Cobb subsequently admitted that he had, in fact, sent Rice the telegrams.

Rice left the Journal in 1905 for the Cleveland News, covering the Cleveland Naps. It was there that he forged a strong friendship with second baseman "Nap" Lajoie. In 1911, the fascination of New York drew Rice to the Evening Mail, where he covered baseball and wrote a column, mixed with liberal portions of his fine poetry. The New York Tribune lured him with an offer of $280.00 a week - a very generous salary for the era. It was at the Tribune that Rice started his syndicated column, "Sportlight" and while most of his energies were directed toward the column, he still reported on major events in fields such as boxing, tennis, golf, football and baseball. As always, his poetry found its way into his sportswriting and he headed his column with verse every day.

Rice moved to the Herald - Tribune and later, the New York Daily News. He continued to write a column and through the Bell Syndicate and the North American Newspaper Alliance, reached newspapers all over the USA and tens of millions of readers. When Rice died in July 1954, he was at his typewriter preparing his column. His deep love of sportswriting is reflected in his own words:

> If somebody whispered to me,
> 'You can have your pick',

If kind fortune came to woo me,
where the gold was thick,
I would still, by hill and hollow,
round the world away,
Stirring deeds of contest follow,
till I am bent and gray.

In 1924, Grantland Rice was given a jewelled gold watch by his peers as "Most Valuable Writer" for his stirring article on the last game of the 1924 World Series in which the Senators' Walter Johnson won the game in relief after he had lost two starts. That gave the Senators a 4 - 3 victory over the Giants - the only World Series won by Washington.

MILTON RICHMAN

Milton Richman was the second of Commissioner Kuhn's "Peerless Journalists" to be given the J. G. Taylor Spink Award in 1980. A hard-working, dedicated writer, he joined the United Press International in 1944 and was constantly in competition with his rival from the Associated Press, Joe Reichler. Richman was equal to the task and won laurels of his own. His scoops included Hank Aaron leaving the Braves for the Milwaukee Brewers after he broke Ruth's home run record, Billy Martin's first signing to manage the Yankees, Pete Rose's signing with the Phillies and "Catfish" Hunter becoming a free agent from the Athletics.

Richman played minor league baseball but quit after he was evaluated as, "Fielding good, running great, hitting pathetic". While serving in the U.S. Army in World War II, Richman did some sportswriting and in 1944 became a member of the UPI staff rising to the position of sports editor/columnist. Known for rarely missing a day on the job, when he did, in fact, miss a single day's work in 1963, a newspaper carried the news of his absence with a one word headline facetiously entitled "GOLDBRICK". Former BBWAA President Ray Kelly Jr. referred to Milton Richman as, "quiet, unassuming, ... with a unique rapport with ballplayers".

DAMON RUNYON

It was 1935, the city was New York, the restaurant Lindy's, and Ed Sullivan the famous variety show host, had just left the two newspapermen. Afterwards, one of the writers said of Sullivan, "That guy can brighten up a room just by leaving it". Over the fifty - odd years since, that line has been oft - repeated but hardly anyone knows that it originated from the mouth of the legendary Damon Runyon, one of the two writers with whom Sullivan had been spending time in Lindy's. In 1967, Damon Runyon was chosen for the J. G. Taylor Spink Award.

Runyon was born in Manhattan, Kansas. He started as a reporter for the <u>Denver Post</u>. In 1920, he moved to the 'eastern Manhattan' and took New York City by storm, joining the <u>New York American</u> of the Hearst chain and within five years became Hearst's brightest luminary as reporter - columnist. Runyon's salary at that time was an incredible $25,000 a year. Runyon was also a prolific short - story and magazine writer and cultivated a wide circle of friends ranging from sports figures to Broadway stars, from journalists to bootleggers and underworld characters. He continued to write until, stricken by throat cancer and in constant pain, he was too weak to hold a pencil.

Damon Runyon's main thrust in the 1930's was in the field of short - story writing. Many of his stories were made into movies. Two of his most beloved works are still favourites today - *Little Miss Marker* starring Shirley Temple and *The Idyll of Miss Sarah Brown*, which lovers of Broadway musical-comedies know better as the critically acclaimed *Guys and Dolls*. Shortly before his death in 1946, Runyon and some friends were standing at the corner of Broadway and 49th Street. As he savoured the theatrical environment he helped to create, unable to speak because of his illness, he whipped out his notepad and wrote, "Listen to the roar". A friend and frequent companion who shared some of Runyon's haunts - actor/comedian Milton Berle - said, "Runyon was in a class by himself, a legend".

Walter Winchell, Runyon's longtime friend and associate, together with other friends, established the Damon Runyon Memorial Cancer Fund. In 1949, the same group of friends put together the Damon Runyon Telethon to raise funds for cancer. Fittingly, Milton Berle served as Master of Ceremonies of the first Telethon. When Winchell died in 1973, his name was added to the fund. The location of the Fund's offices is typical of the zest for life that Runyon and Winchell shared. The address for the Runyon-Winchell Cancer Fund is a town-house on West 56th street that was once a favoured Runyon haunt, the *Club Napoleon*, owned by Runyon's close friend, Owney Madden, a bootlegger.

BUS SAIDT

Bus Saidt joined Leonard Koppett as the 1992 co-winner of the J. G. Taylor Spink Award. An energetic, hard-working journalist, Saidt's schedule was so exacting that most others would have collapsed from sheer exhaustion. He seldom took a plane, yet he was one of the most travelled baseball writers of all time. He would drive from his home in Trenton, New Jersey, to Philadelphia to cover the Phillies, his main beat. When the Phillies were on the road, Saidt worked either Yankees or Mets games.

Saidt started his journalism career as a broadcaster at night while he held a day job as an accountant for the City of Trenton. He held the post of sports director of radio station WBUD from 1947 to 1969. A friend persuaded him to move to the print medium, and he joined the <u>Trentonian</u> in 1964. He switched to the <u>Times of Trenton</u> in 1967 as a sports columnist, remaining with that paper for twenty-two years until his death in 1989.

As a youngster, Bus Saidt played American Legion baseball. That experience imbued him with a profound understanding of, and appreciation for, the subtleties of the game. When he moved to writing about the game, therefore, he did so with unbridled enthusiasm and passion. He revelled in a ball game that was well played, but decried anything that detracted from the game.

Bus Saidt's passion for the national pastime was exceeded only by his love for his profession. Known as "the man from Trenton who never took a day off", he wrote every day. When he did take a day off, he made certain that a column was left for that day. He was admired and respected by colleagues and loved by fans. Even now, several years after his death, he is still missed in Trenton, the city for which he cared so much.

Among the many honours and awards conferred upon Bus Saidt are New Jersey Sportswriter of the Year by the National Sportswriters and Broadcasters Association (three times), New Jersey Press Association and United Press International writing awards. In 1986, he was one of six journalists who received the first Mercer County Media Awards.

H. G. SALSINGER

He was a well - rounded person who was expert in many sports, but never more knowledgeable, never more expert, than in his coverage of baseball and his comments about it. He was a dignified man who brought figurative as well as actual stature into the profession.

These words were uttered by Bob Broeg, Chairman of the Selection Committee of the J. G. Taylor Spink Award, with reference to H. G. Salsinger, the 1968 selection for the Award. Salsinger was born in Springfield, Ohio and spent his early writing years working for newspapers in Springfield, Dayton and Cincinnati. He moved to Detroit, where, for the next fifty years, Salsinger covered baseball and other sports for the <u>Detroit News</u>. A Detroit Tigers fan through and through, Salsinger and the Tigers' Ty Cobb were great friends. He deemed Cobb "the greatest of the great" and in the 1920's, wrote some of the finest biographies of Cobb. Salsinger crusaded for and secured improved working conditions for the media, and left a legacy that makes Detroit one of the best ball clubs in terms of facilities for the working media. Salsinger's interests extended into other areas and he was as expert on wire-haired dogs, rare books, flowers, and paintings as he was in writing about sports.

KEN SMITH

When I met Ken Smith in August 1988, he had been retired for many years and was residing with his wife Emmie in a Cooperstown Nursing Home. Among the prized possessions he showed me was his J. G. Taylor Spink Citation, an award for which he was chosen in 1983, recognition that was long overdue. His retirement as Director of Public Relations of the National Baseball Hall of Fame in 1979 closed the curtain of an association with baseball that lasted for three quarters of a century, dating back to the time he started as a batboy for his home - town team in 1913.

Kenneth Danforth Smith was born in Danbury, Connecticut in 1902. His newspaper coverage of major league baseball started with the <u>New York Graphic</u> in 1925. Two years later, he moved to the <u>New York Mirror</u> where he was assigned to the Giants' beat, a beat he covered for the next thirty years. Smith became a close friend of many of the Giants' players and at one time roomed with the Giants' "Meal Ticket", Carl Hubbell. Despite his closeness to the team, Smith was able to maintain his objectivity as a reporter. Unable to obtain a transfer to the <u>San Francisco Examiner</u> when the Giants moved to San Francisco in 1958, Smith then covered the New York Yankees. At first, his loyalty to the National League made him feel like he was committing treason by switching to an American League club but in time, he adjusted to his new surroundings, developing an affection for the Yankees that rivalled the relationship he had with the Giants.

Ken Smith left the newspaper business to take up an appointment as Director of the National Baseball Hall of Fame and Museum in 1963. He served on Hall of Fame Committees in the early years of the Hall and for many years was Secretary - Treasurer of the BBWAA. His book, "Baseball's Hall of Fame," captures the essence of the inauguration ceremonies of the Hall of Fame in 1939. In his forty years as a baseball writer, Smith developed an acquaintanceship among the baseball fraternity that was without equal. An accomplished accordionist, Ken Smith often made music for his companions in the press box after his task with the typewriter was completed.

"RED" SMITH

Pulitzer prize-winning journalist "Red" Smith[3] had such an impact on American life that when he proposed a boycott of the 1980 Summer Olympics in response to the Soviet invasion of Afghanistan, he triggered widespread discussion which led to the eventual boycott of the games. Smith's presence within his own profession was equally impressive. No less a person than the legendary, Pulitzer prize winner Ernest Hemingway acknowledged that influence in his novel, *Across The River and into the Trees* :

> ... and he noted how the wind was blowing, looked at the portrait, poured another glass of Valpolicella and then started to read the Paris edition of the New York Tribune. `I ought to take the pills, he thought. But the hell with the pills.' "Then he took them just the same and went on reading the New York Herald. He was reading Red Smith and he liked him very much.

Smith shared the 1976 Spink honours with Harold Kaese. Born Walter Wellesley Smith in Green Bay, Wisconsin in 1905, "Red" graduated from the University of Notre Dame with a journalism degree. The first stop on a long

---

3. *Smith won the Pulitzer Prize in 1976, the same year he won the Spink Award.*

journalistic trail was the <u>Milwaukee Sentinel</u> as a cub reporter, followed by the <u>St. Louis Star</u>, moving to the sports department in 1928. At the <u>Star</u> and the <u>Philadelphia Record</u> where he later worked, Smith reported on major events for two decades, including Joe DiMaggio's fifty-six-game hitting streak and Joe Louis' heavyweight championship victory. Smith shared company with two giants of the pressbox - Grantland Rice and Frank Graham - and considered it a privilege to drive them all over the country, as neither Rice nor Graham drove.

The lure of "the Big Apple" drew Smith to the <u>Herald - Tribune</u>, where he worked for twenty-two years, moving rapidly up from beat reporter to columnist. Many people felt that Smith should have used his column to speak out against some of baseball's injustices such as the colour barrier and the reserve clause.[4] In the mid - sixties, Smith went to write for the <u>Herald-Tribune</u>'s archrival, the <u>New York Times</u> where he remained until his death in 1982.

WENDELL SMITH

"I wish I could sign you, too, kid. But I can't." Detroit Tigers scout Wish Egan said these words to nineteen - year old Wendell Smith in 1933, on the day Smith pitched his American Legion team to a 1 - 0 playoff victory. Egan signed Wendell's catcher and the pitcher from the losing team. A victim of baseball's colour line, Smith resolved to work toward the end of such prejudice.

A native of Detroit, Wendell Smith excelled in basketball and baseball in high school and secured an athletic scholarship to West Virginia State College in Charleston. He was campus correspondent for two Charleston newspapers, the <u>Gazette</u> and the <u>Daily Mail</u>, and sports editor of the college paper. Upon graduation in 1937, Smith joined the staff of the country's largest Negro weekly, the <u>Pittsburgh Courier</u> and was promoted to sports editor a year later. At the <u>Courier</u>, he began his drive to get blacks into the Major Leagues.

In 1939, Smith and two prominent blacks - singer Paul Robeson and <u>Courier</u> publisher Ira Lewis - made a presentation to baseball owners, urging them to allow blacks into the Major Leagues. Their plea was simple, "Gentlemen, there is a wealth of baseball talent out there and contrary to what many people say,

---

4.   *Smith did, however, speak out years later, when other writers started to criticize the injustices. Smith felt comfort in numbers.*

we believe these men can play major league baseball and that the majority of the players would tolerate them on their teams." The presentation was met with silence; Commissioner Landis who was present at the meeting and who was himself strongly in favour of maintaining the status quo, did not even respond to the "thank you" letter sent him by the petitioners.

Smith continued his campaign; he interviewed all the National League managers and several high profile players. The managers had no objection to blacks in the Major Leagues, and some like Leo Durocher were very encouraging. About 75% of the players, including Carl Hubbell, Gabby Hartnett and Dizzy Dean, favoured integration. Smith also received support from baseball writers such as Warren Brown and Shirley Povich, although the writers' fraternity as a whole was not supportive. In the meantime, Smith's appliclation for membership in the BBWAA was denied. He conducted most of his interviews from the Schenley hotel where teams stayed when they went to play the Pirates. His articles were well received and several publications picked up his stories.

In 1945 Wendell Smith secured a promise from Pirates owner Bill Benswanger, for scouts to take a look at some Negro League players; Benswanger never kept his promise. Undaunted, Smith plodded on; he obtained a Boston councilman's support and arrangements were made for blacks to tryout with the two Boston teams - the Braves and the Red Sox. Smith chose Jackie Robinson, Sam Jethroe and Marvin Williams. The tryout with the Braves was not held and the Red Sox made a farce of their tryout, matching the three Negro Leaguers against a bunch of high school kids and players from the low minor leagues. Sox officials said the black players looked "like pretty good ballplayers," and promised to contact Smith; they never did.

In the face of mounting frustration, Smith approached Brooklyn Dodgers owner, Branch Rickey who had expressed interest in starting a Negro League of his own. When Rickey finally signed Robinson, he hired Smith ostensibly to scout the Negro Leagues, but in reality to assist in getting Robinson to the Major Leagues. Smith was asked to room with Robinson during road trips in the Minor Leagues.

Smith moved to Chicago in 1947 to work for the <u>Chicago American</u> and finally succeeded in gaining admission to the BBWAA in 1948. He joined WGN - TV in 1964 and remained there up to his death in 1972 at the age of fifty-eight. Ironically, Smith, who was denied membership in the BBWAA on several occasions, eventually became President of the Chicago Press Club. In 1948, he wrote the first biography of Jackie Robinson. He also wrote books for Roy Campanella, Ernie Banks and Joe Louis. A school in Chicago was named in his memory - the Wendell Smith Elementary School.

Wendell Smith was awarded the J. G. Taylor Spink Citation for 1993, the first member of his race to be so honoured.

J. G. TAYLOR SPINK

J.G. Taylor Spink was a true lion of his profession, a man noted for his outstanding service to baseball as well as to the field of journalism. As a tribute to standards for excellence set by Spink throughout his career, the award for excellence in baseball writing was named in his honour and, shortly before his death in 1962, Spink himself was named as the first recipient of the J. G. Taylor Spink Award. The Sporting News, a paper known the "Bible of Baseball", is also part of Spink's legacy to baseball posterity. Founded by Spink's father Charles in 1884, the paper became an internationally respected sports weekly when Spink assumed control of it upon the death of his father in 1914. The paper flourished and Spink became the "unofficial voice of baseball". Players, officials and fans alike looked to him for guidance and leadership.

Taylor Spink never shied away from controversial issues. A strong supporter of the formation of the American League, he criticized the upstart Federal League, and sided with the National League when the fledgling American League raided the Senior Circuit for players. An advocate of corruption - free baseball, he helped ferret out players and gamblers involved in the 1919 Black Sox scandal. Spink welcomed the appointment of Judge Kenesaw Landis as Commissioner of Baseball, and even though the Commissioner was somewhat envious of Spink's wide popularity among the baseball establishment, Spink did not allow that to affect his respect and admiration for Landis.

Spink received numerous awards for his contributions to sport and to American society, including his 1956 citation by both the U.S. Army and Air Force for recognizing and promoting the leisure - time needs of armed service personnel. He also served on a committee on youth fitness. The baseball world admired and respected J. G. Taylor Spink. It was said "...if Spink had not existed, organized baseball would have had to invent him".

J. ROY STOCKTON

J. Roy Stockton was chosen in 1972 to join Dan Daniel and Fred Lieb as recipients of the J. G. Taylor Spink Award. For almost fifty years, Stockton worked as a writer, broadcaster and baseball official. When he retired as sports editor of the St. Louis Post - Dispatch in 1958, Stockton had achieved a reputation as an outstanding sportswriter - a journalist whose razor sharp wit and exceptional writing ability gained him national prominence. He attended Washington University but left before graduating in order to cover a boxing match and spring training baseball in Cuba in 1915. Stockton started a forty - one year association with the Post - Dispatch in 1917, and at the time of his retirement, was sports editor, a position he held for twelve years.

Although primarily a sportswriter - he was President of the BBWAA in 1932 – Stockton also did considerable work on radio, hosting a sports programme for over fifteen years on station KSD in St. Louis. In 1947 , Stockton was part of the first telecast of a baseball game in St. Louis soon after KSD - TV began operating. Following his departure from the Post - Dispatch, Stockton served as President of the Florida State League. Among his other accomplishments are three baseball books, one of which is *The Gas House Gang and a Couple of Other Guys*. Stockton also wrote a series of profiles of baseball personalities for the Saturday Evening Post. He was held in such regard by his colleagues that in 1951, Red Smith of the New York Herald - Tribune proposed that Stockton be considered for the post of Baseball Commissioner to replace A. B. Chandler, describing Stockton as "a man of many gifts and fierce integrity, whose years as one of the country's finest baseball writers have given him a rich background of experience and knowledge."

"DICK" YOUNG

When "Dick" Young was named winner of the 1978 J. G. Taylor Spink Award, he shared the honour with journalist Tim Murnane, a journalist who died in 1917, the year Young was born. Richard Young spent forty-five years as a writer and columnist for the New York Daily News, covering not only baseball but several other sports. Young was also a radio commentator for the New York Jets. A passionate scribe who held strong opinions on a variety of issues, Young wrote without fear of irritating or angering anyone. His mean - spiritedness caused many a feud between himself and prominent sports personalities such as Joe Namath and Howard Cosell. Young also holds the dubious distinction of being responsible for running the lovable Tom Seaver out of New York.

"Dick" Young was, however, a pioneer in baseball journalism, being among the first baseball reporters to invade the clubhouse and bring readers inside stories to complement the results of a baseball game. In the spring of 1987, Young was presented with an award for meritorious service to the game of boxing by the Boxing Writers Association.

CHAPTER XII

THE BROADCASTERS

From the early days of radio to the present 'state of the art' television productions, broadcasters, like writers, have played a significant role in bringing baseball to tens of thousands of fans. This chapter salutes broadcasters who have received the Ford C. Frick Award. It is also a tribute to other fine sportscasters for their contribution in reporting and promoting baseball.

THE FORD C. FRICK AWARD

The Ford C. Frick Award is given to broadcasters, "for major contributions to the game of baseball". Named after former Commissioner Ford Frick, a pioneer broadcaster, the Award was established in 1978 by the National Baseball Hall of Fame. Since then, the honour has been bestowed on an array of distinguished members of the electronic media. Like their counterparts in the print medium, Frick Award winners are not members of the Hall of Fame. They are, however, featured in an exhibit entitled, "Scribes and Mikemen;" the exhibit is housed in the Library and Archive.[1]

MEL ALLEN

"Going, going, gone", and "How about that!" are the trademarks of this co - winner of the first Ford Frick Award in 1978. As the radio and TV voice of the New York Yankees for over two decades, Mel Allen came to be regarded as a symbol of the club and was referred to as "the 10th Yankee". A native of Alabama, Melvin Israel Allen was somewhat of a child prodigy. In elementary school, he skipped grades and at fifteen entered the University of Alabama where he obtained a law degree. Allen played semipro baseball as a centre-fielder and while at university, wrote and edited a sports column for the campus paper, as well as broadcast football games for Alabama. After brief periods as a teacher of public speaking and as a law clerk, Allen joined CBS in New York in 1939, where his first assignment was with station WPIX as part of the team broadcasting Yankees and Giants home games. Allen became chief announcer in 1940 and stayed with WPIX until 1964 except for three years in

---

1.   *Award winners are listed in alphabetical order.*

the Army. The Yankees released him after Ballantine Beer withdrew sponsorship and Allen took on other jobs before joining Sports Channel, where he was back doing Yankees games. Allen has narrated "This Week in Baseball" - a syndicated programme - for several years.

During his time with the Yankees, Allen witnessed and described some of the most magical and dramatic occurrences in the history of the franchise, from Joe DiMaggio's fifty-six-game hitting streak to Don Larsen's perfect game, from Mantle's heroics to Maris' sixty - one home runs. In the same period, Allen shared in the triumph of fourteen Yankees World Series and nineteen pennants.

Mel Allen has received numerous accolades. His voice was used in the Broadway musical "Damn Yankees"; he was presented with a gilded microphone at a function held in his honour; scholarships in Allen's name are awarded by his alma mater and by New York's Geneseo State College.

"RED" BARBER

How often have we heard broadcasters use the phrase "the ducks are on the pond" when the bases are loaded, or heard a hitter described as being "in the catbird seat" when he has a favourable count? These terms have become part of the baseball lexicon, courtesy of "Red" Barber. In 1978, Barber, was named co - winner of the Ford C. Frick Award, joining his friend and co - worker in the broadcast booth, Mel Allen. A native of Mississippi, Barber grew up in Florida and did not hit the big city until he was thirty - one years old in 1939. Walter Lanier Barber broadcast Dodgers games until the club left New York for the West Coast in 1958. In Brooklyn, his Southern accent, distinctive voice and easy flowing delivery endeared him to the people of Flatbush, who regarded him as the voice of the Dodgers. Barber witnessed the advent of Jackie Robinson in 1947, and in later years, prided himself in never referring to Robinson's colour in his broadcasts. Barber teamed up with Mel Allen for several years in covering the World Series but walked away from it in 1953 when the sponsor, Gillette, refused to negotiate the payment for his services.

After the Dodgers departed for the West Coast, Barber covered the Yankees until 1966 when he left New York and returned to Florida. He came out of retirement in 1981 to do the Friday Morning Edition of National Public Radio, from his home in Tallahassee. An upstanding, deeply religious man, "Red" Barber was, ironically, a great admirer of one of baseball's most profane and irascible managers - the late Leo Durocher. Barber respected Durocher's abilities as manager of the Dodgers as well as his sense of fairplay, as shown by the manner in which he dealt with his players' revolt when they heard that Jackie Robinson was moving up to Brooklyn's roster.

JACK BRICKHOUSE

It would take volumes to chronicle the laurels bestowed upon the 1983 Ford C. Frick Award winner, Jack Brickhouse. In a broadcasting career that spanned nearly five decades, Brickhouse demonstrated a versatility that took him into many varied fields from sports to politics, from religion to war. But it was in the sports arena, most notably baseball, that he channelled most of his talents and energies. Ed Stack, President of the Baseball Hall of Fame, in commenting on Brickhouse's selection said, "The name of Jack Brickhouse has always been synonymous with reporting integrity and accuracy ...".

Born in Peoria, Illinois, Brickhouse became the youngest sportscaster in the nation when he started with station WMBD in Peoria in 1934 at the tender age of eighteen. In 1940, he moved to WGN in Chicago, covering the Cubs and the White Sox. Brickhouse spent 1946 behind the microphone for the New York Giants before returning to WGN, where he remained until 1981, the year he stopped doing play - by - play commentary. Later he held the post of Vice - President of the Cubs. When he "hung up his gloves", Brickhouse had called 5,060 games. Brickhouse also worked ballgames for Channel 9 TV in Chicago from the station's first telecast in 1948. By the time he retired, he had televised more baseball games than any other broadcaster. Brickhouse was perhaps equally famous for his twenty - four consecutive years as the play - by - play man for Chicago Bears' games on WGN radio. In addition to several All -Star and World Series games, Brickhouse has covered innumerable games in other sports: All-Star football, NFL Championships, Rose Bowl games, boxing, golf and basketball. When the first telecast was made via satellite in 1962, part of a Cubs/Phillies game was done by Jack Brickhouse.

Brickhouse's versatility was manifest in his work in other areas. During the Vietnam War, he reported from Saigon. He covered Democratic and Republican Conventions, as well as the Inauguration of President Roosevelt in

1945. Brickhouse's interviews included the Archbishop of Canterbury as well as four U.S. Presidents. He also broadcast a papal audience with Pope Paul VI and did "Man On The Street" broadcasts in Japan, England, Iran, France, Hong Kong, Thailand and Germany. Brickhouse is also a noted author whose book, *Thanks For Listening*, was a best seller. He has also written for the <u>Chicago Tribune</u> and <u>Chicago Today</u>. Brickhouse has served in various capacities on numerous boards and organizations, ranging from the Board of Trustees of Illinois Benedictine College and the Chicago Boys Clubs to the NFL Hall of Fame Selection Committee and the Heisman Trophy Selection Committee.

In addition to numerous awards for his work in baseball, Jack Brickhouse has been inducted into a number of sports halls of fame, including the Chicago Cubs HOF, the Chicago Sports HOF, Bradley University HOF, the American Sportscasters HOF and the Peoria Sports HOF. Brickhouse was also named the "Best Sports Announcer" by the American College of Radio Arts and Sciences and was the <u>Chicago Sun Times</u> "Broadcasting's Man of the Year". Brickhouse's scintillating career as a sportscaster is best summed up in his own words, "I regard sports first and foremost as entertainment... I like the `let's go and forget our troubles and have some excitement' approach. I'm convinced you can combine this with integrity and accuracy".

JACK BUCK

John Francis Buck became the eleventh broadcaster to receive the coveted Ford C. Frick Award when he was chosen as the 1987 winner. Buck, a native of Massachusetts, was born in Holyoke in 1924 but grew up in Cleveland, Ohio. In 1943, he enlisted in the U.S. Army and was wounded in battle. On his return, he attended Ohio State University, graduating in radio and speech with a minor in Spanish. While at Ohio State, Buck got his start in broadcasting, working as the play - by - play announcer for Buckeyes football and basketball teams, and later broadcast games for Cardinals farm clubs before joining Harry Caray in the St. Louis booth in 1954. He has spent over four decades as a sportscaster and served as sports director of radio station KMOX in St. Louis.

Buck left KMOX and baseball in 1976 to host NBC's "Grandstand" but later returned to KMOX. Over the years, his stature with the ball club and the fans grew tremendously, earning him the nickname, "The Voice of the Redbirds". The versatile Jack Buck has also worked football, basketball and hockey games, and did play - by - play commentary for the Chicago Bears and the Dallas Cowboys. Buck was honoured by the University of Missouri with a medal from the School of Journalism, and the University of Missouri - St. Louis conferred upon him an honorary degree in humane letters, in recognition of his contribution to the St. Louis Cystic Fibrosis Foundation. He has given much of his time to charities and community projects. An excellent master of ceremonies, Buck was also inducted into the Missouri Sports Hall of Fame.

BUCK CANEL

For five decades, this recipient of the 1985 Ford C. Frick Award took baseball into the homes of Latin Americans and is considered the Dean of the Spanish broadcasters. A native of Argentina, Eli "Buck" Canel was born in Buenos Aires of Scottish - Spanish descent. He was working for the Staten Island Advance in New York when the Associated Press hired him in 1927 as Latin - American correspondent for Central and South America. Seven years later he joined the French wire service, Havas. In 1937, he started a forty-two year association with ABC's Gillette "Cavalcade of Sports" as Spanish broadcaster. Canel was also Spanish announcer for New York Yankees home games, reaching most of the city's two million - plus, Spanish - speaking residents and during the same period, reported on baseball for the French news agency, Agence France Presse.

Buck Canel enjoyed widespread popularity and respect both among his colleagues in the radio booth and in the Spanish - speaking community. His trademark phrase was, "Don't go away, this game is really getting interesting," and he is credited with playing a significant role in the growth of baseball in Latin America. Canel's popularity was underscored in 1959 while he was working in Cuba for NBC. Fidel Castro had just taken over the reins of power and was conducting a news conference for English language media. Castro noticed Canel among the journalists and engaged him in a spirited conversation in Spanish. The other writers became worried over Canel's safety but he told them later that all Fidel wanted to know was why the Milwaukee Braves manager Fred Haney used Lew Burdette instead of Warren Spahn in game seven of the 1958 World Series. The New York Yankees won the game and with it, the World Series.

HARRY CARAY

"An announcer has to be a reporter, a showman and an entertainer" has long been the philosophy of Harry Caray, the 1989 winner of the Ford C. Frick Award. Many people believed that his inclusion among the elite group of Ford Frick honorees was long overdue and that his candour, his belief in free speech and his seeming abrasiveness may have contributed to the delay in his selection. When he finally made it, Caray was the unanimous choice of the selection committee. His career as a major league broadcaster started in St. Louis in 1944 and he remained a Cardinals announcer for twenty - five years. Caray then spent the 1970 season with the Oakland Athletics before moving to Chicago where he worked White Sox games for ten years. In 1981, Caray began broadcasting for the Chicago Cubs where he has remained up to the point of this writing (1994).

In Chicago, Caray's name has become a household word and his trademark "Holy Cow!" is known throughout baseball. He is also famous for leading the fans in rendering, "Take Me Out to the Ball Game," during the seventh inning stretch. A durable sportscaster, Caray never missed a game in forty - three years until he suffered a stroke in 1987. Harry Caray brought baseball to the homes of millions of Americans through his radio broadcasts before the use of television became commonplace. He has epitomized the baseball fan and is highly regarded by fans and journalists alike. Born of Italian parentage - his given surname is Carabina - Caray was inducted into the Italian Hall of Fame in 1989.

BOB ELSON

His friends called him "Commander" and for over five decades, Elson took command of the airwaves as one of the premier sportscasters of his era. So great was the esteem in which he was held, that the U.S. Navy granted him leave so that he could work the 1943 World Series. In 1979, Elson was chosen as the third recipient of the Ford C. Frick Award. Commenting on the selection, Hall of Fame President Ed Stack said, "Bob Elson certainly typifies what this award is all about. His devotion to Baseball and the pleasure he has brought to millions of fans over the years make him a most worthy recipient of this coveted citation."

Elson was behind the microphone for over forty years doing Cubs and White Sox games and spent the 1971 season working Oakland A's games.

Regarded as a pioneer in his field, he conducted the first on - the - field interview in 1931 with Philadelphia Athletics Owner/Manager Connie Mack as the subject. Elson called twelve World Series and nine All-Star games and was twice named "Announcer of the Year" by The Sporting News. In 1976, Elson was invited to the White House to participate in the observance of Baseball's Centennial. A fine public speaker, Bob Elson spent a considerable part of his time away from the radio booth working the banquet circuit. He was also an accomplished interviewer and had a talk show which he conducted from the lobby of the Chicago Theatre.

JOE GARAGIOLA

At a banquet on one occasion, surrounded by the then President of the U.S. Harry Truman, a U.S. Senator and a Governor, Garagiola looked into the camera and said, "Hey, Pop, I just want you to see who I am hangin' out with these days." Later, he told people that his father was in hospital stricken with cancer and he wanted his father to know how grateful he was for the decision to get on the boat and come to America. This proud Italian - American, Joe Garagiola, was cited for the 1991 Ford C. Frick Award. Born in St. Louis, Missouri, as a youngster he played baseball in the streets with Yogi Berra, who went on to become a member of the New York Yankees and a Hall of Famer. Garagiola himself spent nine seasons as a catcher in the Major Leagues with the Cardinals, Pirates, Cubs and Giants.

Garagiola started broadcasting with the St. Louis Cardinals and also broadcast games for the New York Yankees and the Angels. The first telecaster of NBC's "Game of the Week", Garagiola has also worked several World Series and has been a mainstay on NBC's "Today" show. His wit and humour coupled with his knowledge of the game, earned him widespread admiration and respect from baseball fans and sportscasters. He loved to talk and has sometimes been accused of talking too much . He was, however, always fair and informative, often poking fun at himself. Garagiola was honoured for journalistic excellence with the George Foster Peabody and Freedoms Foundation Awards.

CURT GOWDY

A football game played between Pine Bluff and St. Mary's in the freezing cold of Cheyenne, Wyoming in 1944 would hardly be considered a likely spot for the launching of what was to be one of the most outstanding of broadcasting careers. And yet it was there that a Wyoming native, recently discharged from the U.S. Air Force, made his debut as a broadcaster, standing on an orange crate doing the play-by-play of the game. In 1984, this respected and nationally acclaimed sportscaster, Curt Gowdy, was named winner of the Ford C. Frick Award. In 1946, Gowdy moved to Oaklahoma City where he covered basketball, football and baseball. He joined Mel Allen in the Yankees radio booth in 1949 after winning a national audition. Gowdy left New York for Boston in 1951 and for the next fifteen years, covered BoSox games on radio and TV.

While working in Boston Gowdy covered various sports, moving to NBC as Game of the Week announcer in 1966 where he stayed for ten years. As a broadcaster for ABC, Gowdy covered many of the major sporting events - the Super Bowl, the Montreal Olympics, World Series and All - Star games and was the first sportscaster to receive the prestigious George Foster Peabody Award for broadcasting excellence (1970). His Peabody citation read, in part, "...versatility...and blend of reporting, accuracy, knowledge, good humour, infectious honesty and enthusiasm." Gowdy has hosted the American Sportsman series for over twenty years and has served as President of the Basketball Hall of Fame.

MILO HAMILTON

"Today's broadcast must be better than yesterday's" is the credo of the 1992 Ford C. Frick Award honoree, Milo Hamilton. Highly regarded and much-travelled, he has broadcast major league games for six baseball teams, and is now working for his seventh, the Houston Astros, where he has been calling games for nearly a decade.

Hamilton was born in Fairfield, Iowa. He graduated from the University of Iowa, and served in the U. S. Navy during World War II. In Guam, he worked for the Armed Forces Radio Network. His broadcasting career was launched in 1950 when he joined the staff of station KSTT in Davenport, Iowa. He later moved to WTVI in Belleville, Illinois where he was assigned dugout duties for the St. Louis Browns.

Hamilton continued on the move. In 1945, he went to the Cardinals' radio booth when the Browns shifted gears to become the Baltimore Orioles. He also worked for the Chicago Cubs (1955 to 1957, and 1980 to 1984), the White Sox

(1961 to 1965), the Atlanta Braves (1966 to 1975), the Pittsburgh Pirates (1976 to 1979), finally ending up with his present team, the Astros.

Before live radio became common place, Hamilton was involved in the re-creation of many games from the Western Union ticker. Among the memorable games he re-created was the one in which Roger Maris hit his record 61st home run. He was also present and called the double-header in which Stan Musial hit five home runs. He also broadcast live Hank Aaron's 715th home run.

Hamilton credits his success as a broadcaster to his love for the game and the support he has received from legendary broadcasters such as Bob Elson and Jack Brickhouse. His call "Holy Toledo!" is well-known in the eastern and central USA. He believes that despite the widespread use of television, base-ball is enjoyed better on the radio. Television focuses on a single play at a time whereas the radio announcer reports everything that is occurring on the field.

Milo Hamilton devotes much of his spare time to community matters. He has, as Master of Ceremonies, assisted in raising over one and one-half million dollars at charitable functions, dinners and auctions. The Houston Interfaith Charities named Milo "Mr. Sportsman of 1991".

ERNIE HARWELL

He began covering sports in the print medium but moved to the electronic medium where he became one of the premier sportscasters of his era. In 1981 this Washington, Georgia native, Ernie Harwell received the Ford C. Frick Award for his contribution to the National Pastime. Harwell's career started at age fifteen when he obtained a job in the sports department of the Atlanta Constitution, later serving as Atlanta correspondent for The Sporting News. Harwell started his broadcasting career with the Minor League Atlanta Crackers in 1946 and moved up to the Major Leagues in 1948, spending over ten years with the Orioles, the Giants and the Dodgers before joining the Tigers at the end of the 1959 season. For over three decades, Ernie Harwell's voice has been synonymous with Tigers baseball.

Like some of his broadcasting colleagues, Harwell has contributed a num-ber of terms to the baseball lexicon. Among the best-known 'Harwellisms' are "the house by the side of the road", "loooong gone" and "instant runs." And just how often have we heard a broadcaster utter the familiar words "the batter stood at the plate like the house by the side of the road and watched the third strike go by" or that a home run is "loooong gone" or a team that is trailing in the late innings needs "instant runs"?

But Ernie Harwell's accomplishments were not confined to the broadcast booth. A devout Christian, Harwell has played a major role in the advancement of the Baseball Chapel throughout the clubhouses. His love of writing is manifest in the poems he has written, and a number of singers have recorded hits using his lyrics. Ed Stack, President of the Baseball Hall of Fame reflected the sentiments of millions of baseball lovers when he described Harwell as "...kind, polite and pleasant and as venerable as the game itself." Among the memorable plays he has called was Bobby Thomson's "shot heard 'round the world" on October 3, 1951 when the Giants defeated the Dodgers for the National League pennant.

RUSS HODGES

The 1980 recipient of the Ford C. Frick Award, Russ Hodges, is the man whose call of one of the most momentous events in baseball history makes virtually every fan's list of "memorable plays of the game". Russ Hodges was not the only announcer who worked the game that fateful day but it was his voice that was recorded by a fan and preserved for posterity.

The date was October 3,1951. The New York Giants and the Brooklyn Dodgers who had battled tooth and nail down the stretch found themselves with identical 96 - 58 records at the end of the regular season. The rules of the day called for a three - game playoff. The teams split the first two and the deciding game was played at the Giants' Polo Grounds. In the bottom of the ninth, with the Giants trailing 1 - 4, Al Dark and Don Mueller both singled. Whitey Lockman doubled home Dark. Clint Hartung replaced Mueller who sprained his ankle going into third. With two runners on base and one out, Bobby Thomson lined Ralph Branca's second pitch over the left field wall giving the Giants a 5 - 4 victory in what has come to be known as "The Miracle of Coogan's Bluff", named after the bluff overlooking the Polo Grounds. At that moment the crowd went wild. In the broadcast booth, Russ Hodges was equally animated and left this record of the play for baseball: "There's a long fly....It's gonna be...I believe....The Giants win the Pennant! The Giants win the Pennant! The Giants win the Pennant! The Giants win the Pennant! Bobby

Thomson hits into the lower deck of the left field stands! The Giants win the pennant...and they are going crazy!"

Hodges was not merely the man who broadcast that historic game. He was a well -rounded sportscaster who gave up a career in law to become an announcer. He turned to broadcasting after a broken ankle ended his hopes of being a football player while he was on a football scholarship at the University of Kentucky. He broadcast football games and also worked for other radio stations while he took night classes at the University of Cincinnati Law School. Hodges announced games for the Reds, Cubs, White Sox and Senators, and in 1945 went to the Yankees radio booth as Mel Allen's partner. He moved over to cover the Giants in 1948 and moved west with the Giants when they relocated in 1958. Hodges developed a style that was partial to the Giants and answered his critics by saying that a broadcaster could not be detached from players whose strengths and weaknesses he knew so well. Furthermore, Hodges felt that he had an obligation to boost the team for which he worked. His trademark, "Bye - Bye Baby", was used to describe a Giants home run. After four decades as a sportscaster, twenty-two of which were spent with the Giants, Hodges took a position in the Giants public relations department but continued as a part - time broadcaster.

BOB MURPHY

His distinctive midwestern baritone and his call of Roger Maris' 60th home run off Baltimore's Jack Fisher helped him beat out the competition and land him the job as a New York Mets broadcaster. Mets owner Joan Payson, liked Murphy's tape and he was chosen from applicants who submitted some two hundred audio tapes. In 1994, after thirty-two years as a Mets broadcaster, Murphy joined baseball's electronic media elite as a recipient of the Ford C. Frick Award.

An Oaklahoman from Tulsa, Murphy served in the Marines during World War II. On his return to the U.S.A. and needing a job, his brother, Jack Murphy - the sports writer after whom the stadium in San Diego is named - suggested that Bob take up broadcasting. Murphy's sportscasting career began with the Muskogee Reds minor league team. After six years with three minor league teams he moved up to the Major Leagues in 1954, joining the respected Curt Gowdy in the Boston Red Sox radio booth. In 1960, Murphy went to Baltimore where he called Orioles games for two years.

When the expansion New York Mets opened their first season in 1962 Murphy was there along with Hall of Famer Ralph Kiner and Ford Frick Award winner Lindsey Nelson, to call the games. He continued to share duties with Kiner and Nelson on radio and television until 1982 when he was assigned to radio (station WHN) exclusively. Nelson, in the meantime, had moved to San Francisco.

Bob Murphy's dedication to his craft, his thorough knowledge of the game, his wit and friendly style, have endeared him to tens of thousands of fans. His philosophy is akin to that of Satchel Paige's. Paige cautioned, "Don't look back. Something might be gaining on you." Murphy's credo is, "Don't look back over your shoulder. The game is right there in front of you, so I call it as I see it and I don't worry about yesterday's score."

LINDSEY NELSON

The 1988 winner of the Frick Award was known for the pleasant, easy going style, soft southern drawl, as well as a consummate professionalism that made him a most likeable and respected sportscaster. But it was not just his coverage of top sporting events over his long, impressive career that made Nelson one of the most recognised sportscasters of his day. His other trademark was a collection of over three hundred "loud" sports jackets, a collection so distinctive that on one occasion when Nelson was hailing a taxi, the driver recognized him as "the guy with the crazy clothes".

Nelson attended the University of Tennessee, graduating with a major in English. As a youngster, he was a sports reporter for a local newspaper in his hometown Columbia, Tennessee and during the Second World War, served as a correspondent attached to the Ninth Infantry Division, where he spent over four years moving all over Europe and North Africa. Upon returning to the USA, Nelson began broadcasting minor league ball games and set up the sports network for the University of Tennessee. Nelson was an original New York Met, and for seventeen years shared in the team's fortunes, from their beginning in 1962 to their World Championship in 1969. From 1979 to 1981, he announced games for the San Francisco Giants and for the Reds in 1982.

In addition to his baseball duties, Nelson called the NBA "Game of the Week" for six years, NCAA football for fourteen years, Notre Dame football for thirteen seasons, and NFL football on Sunday and Monday for rival net-works for over twenty years. He was also a fixture at the Cotton Bowl for more than twenty - five seasons. A visiting professor of Broadcasting at the University of Tennessee, Nelson has received several prestigious honours and awards, including the Tuss McLaughry Service Award in 1988 and election in 1979 to the National Sportswriters and Sportscasters Hall of Fame.

BOB PRINCE

Bob Prince was an institution in Pittsburgh. In a career that stretched for five decades, he broadcast many sports - boxing, football, hockey - but his forte was baseball. In 1986, he was honoured with the Ford C. Frick Award. The California native originally set out to become a lawyer but abandoned the idea and in 1941 went into broadcasting. He joined the Pirates broadcasting team in the late nineteen forties and spent more than two decades with station KDKA. During this period Prince developed a style that endeared him to fans and players alike: he boosted the team, rooted for the players and made no excuses for being the unabashed head cheerleader of the Pirates. Like Barber and Harwell, Prince introduced several terms to the game: his trademark for a home run was "kiss it good-bye"; "a bug in the rug" was a loose baseball on artificial turf; a close play at first base was "a gnat's eyelash" or "closer than fuzz on a tick's ear"; "a bloop and a blast", meant that the team required two more runs. Prince was also responsible for tagging many of the Pirates with their nicknames: Dave Parker became "The Cobra" and Roberto Clemente, "The Great One."

Prince moved to the Houston Astros after a dispute with KDKA but was rehired shortly before his death in 1985. He worked Monday Night Baseball for ABC and later returned to Pittsburgh where he did Pirates games for tele-vision. But Bob Prince was much more than a fine sportscaster. A great humanitarian, Prince devoted an inordinate amount of time to various charita-ble causes, and all his receipts from speaking engagements were turned over to a school for handicapped children.

His affinity with ballplayers went beyond the confines of the ballpark. In 1971, he arranged for Pirates' pitcher Bruce Kison to fly by helicopter from Baltimore to Pittsburgh after the seventh game of the World Series, in time for Kison's wedding. Prince was so highly regarded by Roberto Clemente that

"The Great One" gave him the silver bat he received for winning the 1961 batting title. Former Pirate General Manager, Joe Brown, described Bob Prince as a man who "had the ability to capture the emotions of Pirate baseball. He showed on -the - air concern and love for the Pirates and the city of Pittsburgh. He was never too busy to help someone else. ... It was his love, his compassion for other people that made him stand out."

BY SAAM

Byrum Saam broadcast over eight thousand major league games for Philadelphia teams over a span of thirty - eight seasons, including the double - header that ended the momentous season of 1941 - the season in which Ted Williams racked up his .406 batting average. Saam worked two World Series (1959 and 1965) and described Jim Bunning's perfect game, as well as twelve other no - hitters. In all those years and with all those historic games to his credit, this lovable, enduring sportscaster was never associated with a winning team. For nearly four decades, Byrum Saam maintained his equanimity, reminding his listeners, "And here we are, rolling along into the eighth inning." He just kept rolling along to the ultimate honour for a baseball announcer, the Ford C. Frick Award, which he won in 1990.

By Saam left his native Texas in 1937 after graduating from Texas Christian University to broadcast college football in Philadelphia. In 1938, he started announcing home games for the Philadelphia Athletics on radio station WCAU and in 1939, took on the Philadelphia Phillies' home games as well. Saam became the full - time play - by - play man for the Athletics in 1950, the year of the "Whiz Kids"[2] when the Phillies won the pennant, just missing being with a winner. When the Athletics left for Kansas City at the end of the 1954 season Saam moved to the Phillies, remaining with the team until 1975 when he retired. In 1976, the Phillies finally won their first divisional title but once again a winner eluded Saam who was in his first year of retirement.

Byrum Saam will be remembered as a durable sportscaster whose deep love for the National Pastime kept him with losing teams for four decades. Day in and day out, Saam gave hope to tens of thousands of Athletics and Phillies

2. *The 1950 Philadelphia Phillies, led by pitcher Robin Roberts, were known as the "Whiz Kids" for their performance on the field. That same year, Saam stopped broadcasting part-time for both the Philadelphia Phillies and the Philadelphia Athletics and became the full-time broadcaster for the Athletics. Ironically, that was the year the Phillies won the pennant.*

fans. Indeed, his occasional slip of the tongue seems to have added to his charm rather than detract from it. Among Saam's memorable Freudian slips; "Alex Johnson is going back...back. His head hits the wall. He reaches down, picks it up, and throws it into second base," and "Good afternoon, By Saam, this is everyone speaking."

VIN SCULLY

The Ford C. Frick Award for 1982 went to the eloquent Dodgers' broadcaster Vincent Scully. Scully's masterful command of the English language, mellifluous delivery and thorough grasp of the game of baseball have made him one of the most respected members of his profession and earned him the admiration of Dodgers fans. In fact, Dodgers fans so admired Scully that in 1976 they voted him the "Most Memorable Personality" in Los Angeles Dodgers baseball history.

Scully was a Fordham University graduate and in 1950 joined the eminent "Red" Barber in the Brooklyn Dodgers broadcast booth. When the lovable "Bums" moved to the West Coast Scully moved as well, later becoming the number one announcer. He has also covered baseball and golf for NBC TV and has broadcast several World Series and All - Star games. Among the events Scully broadcast to the world were Don Larsen's World Series perfection in 1956, Henry Aaron's 715th home run, Maury Wills' 104 stolen bases in 1962, and Don Drysdale's fifty-eight scoreless innings. Scully has received the "Outstanding Sportscaster Award" (given by the National Sportscasters and Sportswriters Association) three times and has also been honoured as the "Sportscaster of the Year" by the American Sportscasters Association and "Broadcaster of the Year" by the Southern California Broadcasters' Association.

CHUCK THOMPSON

His dulcet tones, his grammatical precision, and his ability to describe the unfolding of a play on the field, prompted someone more than a decade ago to suggest that the voice of Chuck Thompson "be bronzed and preserved for the ages". In 1993, Chuck Thompson was honoured with the Ford C. Frick Award.

His broadcasting career started in an unusual way. Chuck had gone to a radio station in Reading, Pennsylvania to audition for a singing part but ended up as a summer intern. Later, in 1941, he became a full-time announcer with WIBG in Philadelphia. Thompson joined the Philadelphia Phillies broadcasting team upon his return from military service in 1946.

Radio Appreciation Day at Shibe Park in 1946 was an especially momentous one for Chuck Thompson. Between games of a double-header the regular Phillies play-by-play broadcasters were honoured on the field. They were unable to get back to the radio booth in time to call the second game. Thompson, alone in the booth, sized up the situation and took over the microphone. He performed so splendidly that he was hired to broadcast Phillies and Athletics games in 1947 and 1948.

Thompson moved to Baltimore in 1949 to become chief broadcaster of the International League AAA Orioles. When Baltimore rejoined the American League in 1954, Thompson moved up with the team. Apart form a four-year break calling Washington Senators games, he has been calling Orioles games ever since.

Thompson who also broadcast games for the Baltimore Colts of the NFL, is adored in Baltimore. He has two trademarks — his hat, and his exclamation "Ain't the beer cold!" when the Orioles are in an advantageous position.

EPILOGUE

THE 1993 INDUCTION CEREMONIES

The 1993 Induction Ceremonies were a resounding success. Returning Hall of Famers surpassed the 1992 attendance as thirty-seven of them came to welcome Reggie Jackson into their fraternity. About twelve-thousand pilgrims journeyed to Cooperstown to pay homage to baseball's immortals and to witness the anointing of "Mr. October", Reggie Jackson. The lawns of the Alfred Corning Clark Gymnasium afforded ample space for fans to watch the Induction Ceremonies.

Reggie delivered a dynamic speech in which he paid tribute to the National Pastime and expressed thanks to the people who helped him along the road to baseball immortality. His eloquence prompted one New York City newspaperman the very next day to write a column urging the baseball establishment to give serious consideration to Jackson in its search for a new Commissioner of Baseball.

Also honoured were three members of the media. Leonard Koppett of the New York Times and Bus Saidt of the Trenton Times (posthumously) received the Spink Citation; Chuck Thompson — the Voice of the Orioles — was presented with the Ford C. Frick Award. The Hall of Fame game between the Los Angeles Dodgers and the Cleveland Indians was rained out. Two autograph sessions, organized by the Hall of Fame and co-sponsored by Leaf-Donruss, enabled youngsters to meet Hall of Famers and collect their autographs.

THE 1994 INDUCTION CEREMONIES

Thirty - four returning Hall of Famers and over twelve thousand fans witnessed the enshrinement of three new members into the National Baseball Hall of Fame. Steve Carlton, elected in his first year of elegibility, was the sole choice of the Baseball Writers' Association of America (BBWAA); Phil Rizzuto and Leo Durocher were named by the Veterans' Committee. Their selection was long overdue. Durocher was inducted posthumously.

New York Mets broadcaster Bob Murphy, received the Ford C. Frick Award and the late Wendell Smith who wrote for the Chicago American and the Sun-Times, was awarded the J. G. Taylor Spink Citation.

The Seattle Mariners and the Philadelphia Phillies participated in the Hall of Fame game in Doubleday Field, with the Mariners emerging victors, 4 - 3.

The National Baseball Hall of Fame continues to attract visitors in droves. It enjoys a popularity unequalled among institutions of its kind and is a source of immeasurable pleasure and wonderment for the casual baseball fan as well as the serious student of the history of the game. It remains the magnet that attracts me every summer to its hallowed halls and to the Induction Ceremonies.

THE PRESENT AND THE FUTURE; GRAMPA AND GRANDSON - 1991

APPENDIX A:

An Insider's Guide to Cooperstown

This "Insider's Guide" is intended to assist the prospective visitor in planning a trip to Cooperstown. It focuses primarily on the annual Hall of Fame Induction Ceremonies but would be equally useful for visitors all year round. At the end of this "Guide" is a list of publications which contain information regarding accommodation, food, entertainment, recreation and other facilities and services that the visitor to Cooperstown might require.

In early January, the Baseball Writers' choices for induction into the Hall of Fame are announced. At the same time the date for the Induction Ceremonies is set - usually the last Sunday in July or the first Sunday in August.

Accommodation should be reserved early. It is easy to find lodgings in Cooperstown for most of the year. However, during the months of July and August and especially during the week around the Induction, space is at a premium and unprepared visitors to the Induction will often find themselves hunting for a place to stay in neighbouring towns and villages.

As the date of departure to Cooperstown approaches, check to ensure that all arrangements are in order. Visitors from outside the U.S.A. should pay attention to such health and immigration requirements as vaccinations and visas. Canadian visitors have to provide only identification - a passport or birth certificate or Immigration Identification card.

The Attractions of Cooperstown

On arrival in Cooperstown it is advisable to make a brief tour to orient yourself. This tour will help you identify key points and will save you time during the hectic Induction weekend. Here are a few places that should be included in your tour:

Chamber of Commerce Office: Located at 31 Chestnut Street, the office contains a large selection of brochures, booklets and other publications on Cooperstown. Courteous, professional staff are on hand to answer enquiries and assist in locating accommodation, etc. The office is open throughout the year.

<u>Doubleday Field</u>: Doubleday Field is situated behind the Chamber of Commerce office, to the east of Chestnut Street and south of Main Street. This spot was once a cow pasture belonging to farmer Elihu Phinney and is the site, reputedly, upon which the first recorded baseball game in the U.S.A. was played in 1839. That game, legend has it, was organized by Abner Doubleday.

Doubleday Field has dimensions similar to major league ballparks. Behind homeplate is a small, covered structure with seats reserved for dignitaries. A dugout, tiny by major league proportions, is located below this section. Open stands run along the left and right sides of the field.

<u>Doubleday Plaza</u>: To the north of Doubleday Field, facing Main Street, is a parking lot. To its right and left are the shops that comprise Doubleday Plaza. Among these shops is "Baseball Nostalgia", a store which contains a variety of baseball-related items and the Doubleday Batting Range, in which visitors can take swings at a baseball or test their pitching skills.

<u>National Baseball Hall of Fame and Museum, Inc.</u>: The Hall is open all year round, except for Thanksgiving, Christmas and New Year's. Hours are 9:00 a.m. to 9:00 p.m., May 1 to September 30 and 9:00 a.m. to 5 p.m. October 1 to April 30. Admission charges are $8.00 (U.S.) for adults and $3.00 (U.S.) for juniors (ages 7 to 12). For your convenience, a map with the layout of the Museum follows:

GUIDE TO EXHIBITS

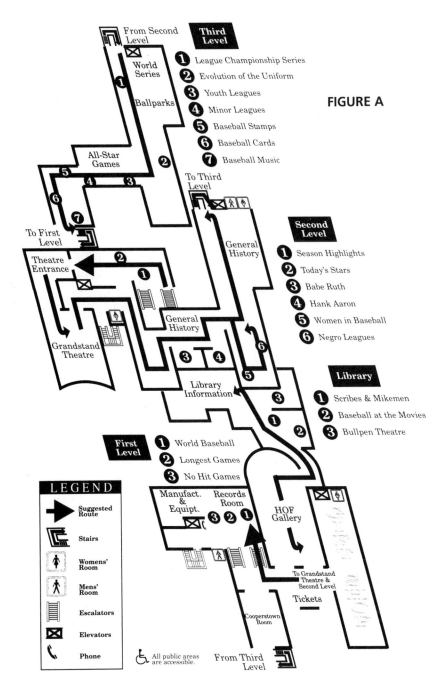

Third Level

1. League Championship Series
2. Evolution of the Uniform
3. Youth Leagues
4. Minor Leagues
5. Baseball Stamps
6. Baseball Cards
7. Baseball Music

FIGURE A

From Second Level

World Series

Ballparks

All-Star Games

To First Level

Theatre Entrance

Grandstand Theatre

General History

To Third Level

General History

Library Information

Second Level

1. Season Highlights
2. Today's Stars
3. Babe Ruth
4. Hank Aaron
5. Women in Baseball
6. Negro Leagues

Library

1. Scribes & Mikemen
2. Baseball at the Movies
3. Bullpen Theatre

First Level

1. World Baseball
2. Longest Games
3. No Hit Games

Manufact. & Equipt.

Records Room

HOF Gallery

To Grandstand Theatre & Second Level

Tickets

Cooperstown Room

From Third Level

LEGEND

➤ Suggested Route

Stairs

Womens' Room

Mens' Room

Escalators

Elevators

Phone

All public areas are accessible.

<u>Alfred Corning Clark (ACC) Gymnasium</u>: Located on Lower Susquehanna Avenue, about five minutes drive from the Hall of Fame, the Gymnasium is surrounded by several acres of lawn. Facilities include swimming pools, an aerobics studio, gym floor, racquetball and squash courts, saunas, a cafe and a bowling alley. Open daily from 6:30 a.m. to 10:30 p.m., September to May, and to 9:30 p.m., June to August, the Gymnasium caters to residents and to visitors. The Hall of Fame Induction Ceremonies moved from Cooper Park to the south lawn of the ACC Gymnasium in 1992. For further information, call (607) 547-2800.

<u>Fenimore House</u>: Fenimore House Museum is the Headquarters of the New York State Historical Association. Its three floors contain folk art, academic and decorative art, and a fine collection of life masks of early Americans such as John Adams and Thomas Jefferson, as well as James Fenimore Cooper memorabilia. Fenimore House is situated about one mile outside Cooperstown on Route 80, along the shore of Lake Otsego. Admission fees are $7.00 (US) for adults and $2.50 (U.S.) for juniors. Fenimore House is open as follows: May / September 6 to October 31 (daily), 10:00 a.m. to 4:00 p.m.: June / September 5 (daily), 9:00 a.m. to 5:00 p.m.: November / December (closed Mondays); 10:00 a.m. to 4:00 p.m.: For information on opening hours at other times call (607) 547-2533.

<u>Farmers' Museum</u>: The Farmers' Museum and Village Crossroads are located across the road from Fenimore House on Route 80. Exhibits featuring farm, home and craft history, highlight life in rural upstate New York during the Revolutionary (1775-1783) and Civil (1861-1865) Wars. Comprised of a main barn and twelve historic buildings, the Museum is staffed by people in period costumes and demonstrations of various functions such as weaving, cooking, and blacksmithing, are carried out continually.

Also housed in the Farmers' Museum is the famous "Cardiff Giant", a huge figure of a man made from granite. This figure was once passed off as the preserved body of a giant human and was later exposed as a "giant" hoax. Admission to the Museum is $8.00 (U.S.) for adults and $3.00 (U.S.) for juniors. Museum hours are 10:00 a.m. to 4:00 p.m., April / November to December (closed Mondays); 10:00 a.m. to 4:00 p.m. May / September 6 to October 31;

9:00 a.m. to 5:00 p.m. June to September 5. Call (607) 547-2533 for operating hours during the remaining months.

Combinations of tickets for the Hall of Fame, Fenimore House and Farmers' Museum are available as follows:

	Adult	Junior
• Baseball Hall of Fame and Fenimore House -	$11.00	$4.50
• Baseball Hall of Fame and Farmers' Museum -	$13.00	$5.00
• Fenimore House and Farmers' Museum -	$11.00	$4.50
• Three-way Tickets (all Museums) -	$17.50	$7.00

Rates are subject to change.

Lake Otsego Boat Tours: Each boat tour lasts approximately one hour and a tour guide gives a running commentary of points of interest as the tour progresses. Two yachts, the *Chief Uncas* and the *Narra Mattah*, which sailed Lake Otsego at the turn of the century, have been restored and are used for the tours. Operating everyday from May 15, to October 12, boats leave the Fair Street dock at 10:00 a.m., 11:00 a.m., 1:00 p.m., 2:00 p.m., 3:00 p.m., 4:00 p.m. and 6:00 p.m. Boat tour prices are $8.50. Charter and catering rates are available upon request - call (607) 547-8238 or 547-6031. For general information write Captain Lyman Bass Townsend, P.O. Box 644, Cooperstown, New York, USA, 13326 or call (607) 547-5295.

As well as the attractions listed above the visitor can find opera, theatre, art galleries, golf courses, recreation areas and camp grounds, and other museums.

Weather in Cooperstown

The following chart gives the visitor a good idea of the temperature to expect when visiting Cooperstown at various times of the year:

WEATHER IN COOPERSTOWN[1].			
	AVG. LOW	**AVG. HIGH**	**AVG. MONTHLY**
January	10.9	30.5	20.8
February	12.4	33.1	22.8
March	21.1	41.0	31.1
April	32.0	56.0	44.0
May	41.0	67.5	54.3
June	50.7	76.5	63.6
July	55.1	80.5	67.8
August	53.5	78.5	66.0
September	47.2	71.7	59.4
October	37.2	61.5	49.4
November	28.9	46.5	37.7
December	17.4	34.3	25.9

1.   All temperature in degrees Fahrenheit.

Source: Mark Hanok of <u>Exacta-Weather</u>, P.O. Box 931, Oneonta, N.Y., 13820. Call (607) 988-6391.

FIGURE B

Induction Ceremonies

For visitors who go to Cooperstown for the Hall of Fame Induction Ceremonies, the following additional tips will enhance the quality of the visit.

Autographs: One hour autograph sessions are usually scheduled during the weekend and require registration, as a limited number of fans are allowed to each of the sessions. Information can be obtained at the Hall of Fame. The sessions which are free of charge, are sponsored by a major baseball card company and are organized and supervised by the Hall of Fame.

Friends of the Hall of Fame: Learn more about the Hall of Fame while at the same time supporting it by becoming a "Friend of the Hall of Fame". In return for a membership fee, renewed annually, members receive a pass to the Hall of Fame, the Yearbook, a T-shirt, a decal and four newsletters. For further information, call (607) 547-9988 or write to:

> National Baseball Hall of Fame and Museum, Inc.
> Fan Club Department,
> P.O. Box 590F,
> Main Street,
> Cooperstown, New York, 13326

Hall of Fame Cachets: On Induction Day, cachets are put on sale in the Gift Shop. These are specially made legal-sized envelopes with distinctive decorations featuring the inductees.

Hall of Fame Game: On Monday, a Hall of Fame game is played in Doubleday Field. Major League teams from the American and National Leagues participate in the game which starts in the early afternoon. Tickets for the game go on sale in May by telephone or in person through Ticketmaster outlets in the Northeastern United States and Southern Ontario. Doubleday Field has a seating capacity of slightly under ten-thousand.

Hall of Fame Supplement: A local newspaper, the _Daily Star_, publishes a special Hall of Fame insert. Sold for $1.00, this supplement contains a great deal of information on the Hall of Fame and the immortals enshrined therein.

Hall of Fame Yearbook: Also on sale at the Hall of Fame Gift Shop is the Yearbook. It contains personal and statistical information, and portraits of all Hall of Fame members, as well as information on the Hall of Fame and the Library.

Inductee Postcards: After the Induction Ceremonies, postcards of the newly-enshrined members are sold in the Hall of Fame Gift Shop. Cost is $ 0.25 each. These are reproductions of Hall of Fame plaques and feature the portrait as well as highlights of each inductee's career. Postcards of all the other immortals are also on sale.

Induction Ceremonies: The Induction Ceremonies are held on the Sunday of the Induction weekend. Although the Ceremonies do not start until 2:30 p.m., people start gathering from early morning, often as early as 5:30 a.m. By the time the actual proceedings begin, the crowd can grow to about ten-thousand and has sometimes reached fifteen-thousand, depending on who is being inducted, as well as other factors such as anniversaries. In 1989, for example, two popular players, Johnny Bench and Carl Yastrzemski, were among those inducted. The popularity of the two players, coupled with the fact that both played for teams within a day's driving distance from Cooperstown and with the observance of three anniversaries - the 50th Anniversary of the Hall of the Fame, the 150th Anniversary of the first recorded baseball game, and the 200th Anniversary of James Fenimore Cooper - caused attendance at the 1989 Ceremonies to exceed fifteen-thousand.

In 1992, the Induction Ceremonies were moved to the south lawn of the Alfred Corning Clark (A.C.C.) Gymnasium where there is ample room to accommodate large crowds and meet future demands for space. A covered platform is provided for the inductees and Hall of Famers who come back every year to welcome the new inductees to their ranks. Loudspeakers are placed throughout the lawn so that fans can hear as well as see the proceedings. The Ceremonies last about two hours.

Induction Day Covers: Sidewalk vendors sell Induction Day covers for $2.00 to $5.00. These envelopes are adorned with colourful miniature pictures of inductees. By affixing postage stamps on the envelopes, fans can have them cancelled with the Induction Day hand stamp at the Post Office, across the street from the Hall of Fame.

Game Day Covers: Envelopes adorned with the logos of the two teams playing in the Hall of Fame game, are also on sale. The Post Office offers a Game Day cancellation service similar to that offered on Induction Day.

Induction Day Bats: Each year, approximately five-hundred Induction Day bats go on sale the Saturday of the Induction weekend. The sale starts at 8:30 a.m. in the Hall of Fame Gift Shop. In order to be eligible to purchase a bat, a ticket must be obtained from Hall of Fame employees who distribute the tickets to those in the "bat line". Bats are limited to one per person.

Souvenir Programme: Published by *The Sporting News*, this magazine is given out free of charge on Induction Day. It contains a schedule of events, articles, statistics on those to be inducted, information on recipients of media awards and an alphabetical listing of Hall of Fame members. Many fans attach postage stamps to the front cover of the programme and have these cancelled with the Induction Day hand stamp at the Post Office. This service is performed voluntarily by postal employees in the Cooperstown Post Office on Main Street.

Miscellaneous: A variety of other items are also on sale. These include lithographs of those inducted over the weekend, photographs, baseball cards, T-shirts, pins, buttons, books and magazines. Prices vary.

Publications

The following publications will aid in the smooth planning of a trip to Cooperstown and the Hall of Fame:

(i) <u>Cooperstown Area Guide</u>: Published annually by the Chamber of Commerce, this guide lists all the facilities and services available in the Village, ranging from eateries and accommodations (including campgrounds) to shopping and attractions, from places of worship to hospitals. Maps are included. A copy may be obtained by writing to the Cooperstown Chamber of Commerce, 31 Chestnut Street, Cooperstown, New York, 13326 or by calling (607) 547-9983. There is no charge for the guide.

(ii) <u>New York Tour Book</u>: Published by the American Automobile Association (AAA), this book is free to AAA or Canadian Automobile Association (CAA) members. It lists accommodations, restaurants, attractions, etc. throughout the State of New York. Copies may be obtained at local CAA or AAA branches.

(iii) <u>Otsego</u>: This magazine is published annually and focuses on the area known as Otsego County. It features information similar to that provided by the Cooperstown Area Guide. Copies may be obtained by writing to Otsego Books, P.O. Box 202, Laurens, New York, 13796. Include $1.00 in stamps.

APPENDIX B:

Services Offered by the National Baseball Library & Archive

History of the Library

The National Baseball Library was opened in 1939. It was located in the Hall of Fame Museum building until 1968 when it was moved to its present quarters behind the Hall of Fame in Cooper Park. The Library is open to the public from 9:00 a.m. to 5:00 p.m., Monday to Friday, all year round except for national holidays. During the months of June, July and August, the Library is open on Saturdays and Sundays for casual visitors. A professional librarian and several researchers are on hand to assist visitors with their research and enquiries. It is advisable to make appointments well in advance owing to limited study space.

The Library is a non-profit organization. Like the Hall of Fame, the Library relies on the goodwill of players and their families, fans and collectors, for items to enhance its collections. Through the generosity of these donors[1], the Library has become the repository of the largest collection found anywhere in the world of material pertaining to baseball. Among the services offered are the following:

- *Collections:* Included in this category are books, periodicals, documents, newspapers, media guides, team publications, biographical files, player records, subject files, scrapbooks, boxscores, statistics, correspondence, autographs, scorecards, programmes, schedules, cartoon art, poetry, sheet music, phonograph records, audio recordings, film, video recordings and microfilm.

- *Geneology:* This includes biographical information on major league players, managers, coaches, umpires, executives, broadcasters, sportswriters and other baseball personalities. Some information on minor league players is also available.

- *Photo Reproduction:* For a fee, you can have black and white or colour reproductions made from some 150,000 photographs of players, teams, stadia and events.

---

1. *Those wishing to make a donation may contact the Librarian. Copies of documents, photographs, etc., are accepted in cases where originals cannot be donated. Special recognition and privileges are accorded those whose articles are accepted by the Library.*

- *Photocopy:* Again, for a small fee, photocopies of documents may be obtained.

Services are available in person, over the telephone or through the mail. Write to:

> The Librarian
> National Baseball Hall of Fame and Museum, Inc.,
> P.O. Box 590
> Cooperstown, New York, U.S.A. 13326
> Or telephone (607) 547-2101

APPENDIX C:

Criteria for Election to the Hall of Fame

Rules for Election

Rules for Election to The National Baseball Hall of Fame by Members of The Baseball Writers' Association of America

1. Authorization - By authorization of the Board of Directors of the National Baseball Hall of Fame and Museum, Inc., the Baseball Writers' Association of America (BBWAA) is authorized to hold an election every year for the purpose of electing members to the National Baseball Hall of Fame from the ranks of retired baseball players.

2. Electors - Only active and honorary members of the Baseball Writers' Association of America, who have been active baseball writers for at least ten (10) years, shall be eligible to vote. They must have been active as baseball writers and members of the Association for a period beginning at least ten (10) years prior to the date of election in which they are voting.

3. Eligible Candidates - Candidates to be eligible must meet the following requirements:
   (A) A baseball player must have been active as a player in the Major Leagues at some time during a period beginning twenty (20) years before and ending five (5) years prior to election.
   (B) Player must have played in each of ten (10) Major League championship seasons, some part of which must have been within the period described in 3 (A).
   (C) Player shall have ceased to be an active player in the Major Leagues at least five (5) calendar years preceding the election but may be otherwise connected with baseball.
   (D) In case of the death of an active player or a player who has been retired for less than five (5) full years, a candidate who is otherwise eligible shall be eligible in the next regular election held at least six (6) months after the date of death or after the end of the five (5) year period, whichever occurs first.
   (E) Any player on Baseball's Ineligible list shall not be an eligible candidate.

4. Method of Election
   (A) BBWAA Screening Committee - A Screening Committee consisting of baseball writers will be appointed by the BBWAA. This Screening Committee shall consist of six members, with two members to be elected at each Annual Meeting for a three-year term. The duty of the Screening Committee shall be to prepare a ballot listing in alphabetical order eligible candidates who (1) received a vote on a minimum of five percent (5%) of the ballots cast in the preceding election or (2) are eligible for the first time and are nominated by any two of the six members of the BBWAA Screening Committee.
   (B) An elector will vote for no more than ten (10) eligible candidates deemed worthy of election. Write-in votes are not permitted.
   (C) Any candidate receiving votes on seventy-five percent (75%) of the ballots cast shall be elected to membership in the National Baseball Hall of Fame.

5. Voting - Voting shall be based upon the player's record, playing ability, integrity, sportsmanship, character, and contributions to the team(s) on which the player played.

6. Automatic Elections - No automatic elections based on performances such as a batting average of .400 or more for one (1) year, pitching a perfect game or similar outstanding achievement shall be permitted.

7. Time of Election - The duly authorized representatives of the BBWAA shall prepare, date and mail ballots to each elector no later than the 15th day of January in each year in which an election is held. The elector shall sign and return the completed ballot within twenty (20) days. The vote shall then be tabulated by the duly authorized representatives of the BBWAA.

8. Certification of Election Results - The results of the election shall be certified by a representative of the Baseball Writers' Association of America and an officer of the National Baseball Hall of Fame and Museum, Inc. The results shall be transmitted to the Commissioner of Baseball. The BBWAA and National Baseball Hall of Fame and Museum, Inc. shall jointly release the results for publication.

9. Amendments - The Board of Directors of the National Baseball Hall of Fame and Museum, Inc. reserves the right to revoke, alter or amend these rules at any time.

Rules for Election to The National Baseball Hall of Fame by Members of Baseball Hall of Fame Committee on Baseball Veterans

1. Name - The Committee shall be known as the BASEBALL HALL OF FAME COMMITTEE ON BASEBALL VETERANS.

2. Number - The Committee shall consist of eighteen (18) members: namely a Chairman and seventeen (17) members. Membership of this Committee shall consist of (a) six (6) former baseball players who are members of the National Baseball Hall of Fame, (b) six (6) individuals who are members of the Baseball Writers' Association of America and/or have experience as baseball broadcasters and (c) six (6) individuals now or formerly connected with baseball, but not from (a) or (b) above. An officer of the National Baseball Hall of Fame and Museum, Inc. shall act as non-voting Secretary.

3. Method of Appointment - The Committee shall be appointed by the Board of Directors of the National Baseball Hall of Fame and Museum, Inc. who shall have the sole power to fill all vacancies caused by the expiration of the term of an appointment, death, physical or mental incapacity, resignation or failure to perform the duties assigned to the Committee or to participate in its activities.

4. Term - The term of each appointment is for six (6) years and expires on the date of the election of a successor or on December 31st of the year on which the appointment expires whichever is earlier.

5. Duties - The Committee shall consider all eligible candidates and hold elections every year. It shall have such further duties as may be assigned to it from time to time by the Board of Directors of the National Baseball Hall of Fame and Museum, Inc.

6. Eligible Candidates - Candidates to be eligible must be selected from:
   (A) Major league players who have competed in any portion of at least ten (10) championship seasons and who have been retired as players for at least twenty-three (23) years. Candidates whose careers began after 1945 are eligible for consideration if they meet one of the following criteria: (1) Received votes on at least sixty percent (60%) of the ballots cast in any one election of the Baseball Writers' Association of America

(BBWAA); (2) Received votes on at least one hundred (100) of the ballots cast in any one of the Baseball Writers' Association of America elections prior to February 4, 1991.

(B) Baseball Executives and/or Managers and/or Umpires who have been retired from organized baseball as Baseball Executives and/or Managers and/or Umpires for at least five (5) years prior to the election (the five (5) year waiting period shall be reduced to six (6) months for anyone who has reached the age of sixty-five (65)) and players who played in any portion of at least ten (10) years in the Negro Baseball Leagues prior to 1946 or whose service in the Negro Baseball Leagues prior to 1946 and in the Major Leagues thereafter totals at least ten (10) years or portions thereof.

(C) Those whose careers involved stints as both players and managers/executives/umpires may be considered for their overall contributions to the game; however, the specific category in which such individuals shall fall for purposes of election shall be determined by the role in which they were most prominent. A "player" must fulfill the requirements in 6 (A).

(D) No member of the Baseball Hall of Fame Committee on Baseball Veterans can be elected to the National Baseball Hall of Fame while a member of the Committee.

(E) Any person on Baseball's ineligible list shall not be an eligible candidate.

7. Number to be Elected - The Committee is authorized to elect each year a maximum of one (1) member from those eligible under Paragraph 6 (A), and a maximum of one (1) member from those eligible under Paragraph 6 (B).

8. Time and Place of Election - Elections shall be held annually no later than March 15 at such time and place as the Chairman of the Baseball Hall of Fame Committee on Baseball Veterans may designate after consultation with the President of the National Baseball Hall of Fame and Museum, Inc.

9. Voting - Voting shall be based upon the individual's record, ability, integrity, sportsmanship, character and contribution to the game.

10.Method of Election

    (A) Screening Committee - A screening committee consisting of six (6) members of the Baseball Hall of Fame Committee on Baseball Veterans shall be appointed by the Committee Chairman to serve three year terms. The duty of the screening committee shall be to prepare two ballots of eligible candidates, who must be nominated by at least two (2) of the six (6) screening committee members. One ballot shall contain twenty (20) candidates from Paragraph 6 (A) and the second ballot twenty (20) candidates from Paragraph 6 (B).

    (B) Meeting for Purpose of Election

        1. A quorum will consist of two-thirds of the total membership of the committee. No proxies are permitted.

        2. Separate votes will be taken on those eligible under Section 6, Paragraph (A) and under Section 6, Paragraph (B).

        3. Each committee member may vote for a maximum of ten (10) eligible candidates. The one receiving the most votes will be elected provided the candidate has been named on 75% of the ballots cast. In the event no one is elected on the first ballot, a second ballot listing the first ballot's top ten (10) vote getters shall be prepared and presented. Each committee member in attendance may vote for a maximum of five (5) eligible candidates appearing on the second ballot. The one receiving the most votes will be elected provided the candidate has been named on 75% of the ballots cast.

        4. No additional ballots shall be taken regardless of the results of the first and second ballots.

11. Minutes - The Committee shall keep minutes of its meetings, one copy of which is to be placed on file at the National Baseball Hall of Fame Museum, Inc.

12. Automatic Elections - No automatic elections based on performances such as batting average of .400 or more for one (1) year, pitching a perfect game or similar outstanding achievement shall be permitted.

13. Amendments - The Board of Directors of the National Baseball Hall of Fame and Museum, Inc. reserves the right to revoke, alter or amend these rules at any time.

COOPERSTOWN BUSINESS DISTRICT

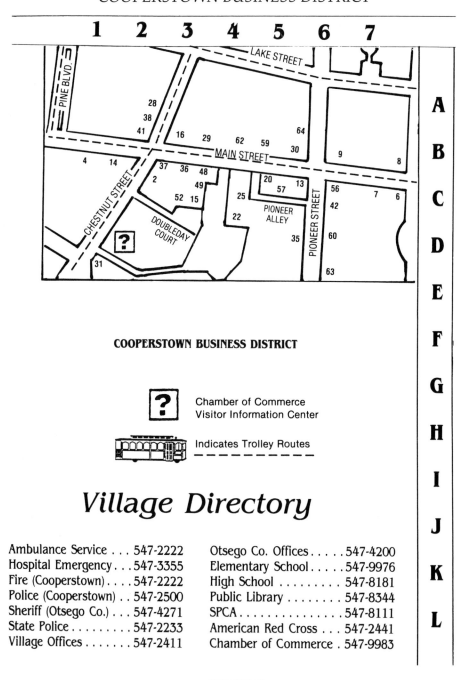

COOPERSTOWN BUSINESS DISTRICT

? Chamber of Commerce
Visitor Information Center

Indicates Trolley Routes

Village Directory

Ambulance Service . . . 547-2222	Otsego Co. Offices 547-4200
Hospital Emergency . . . 547-3355	Elementary School 547-9976
Fire (Cooperstown) 547-2222	High School 547-8181
Police (Cooperstown) . . 547-2500	Public Library 547-8344
Sheriff (Otsego Co.) . . . 547-4271	SPCA 547-8111
State Police 547-2233	American Red Cross . . . 547-2441
Village Offices 547-2411	Chamber of Commerce . 547-9983

FIGURE C

APPENDIX E:

MAP OF COOPERSTOWN

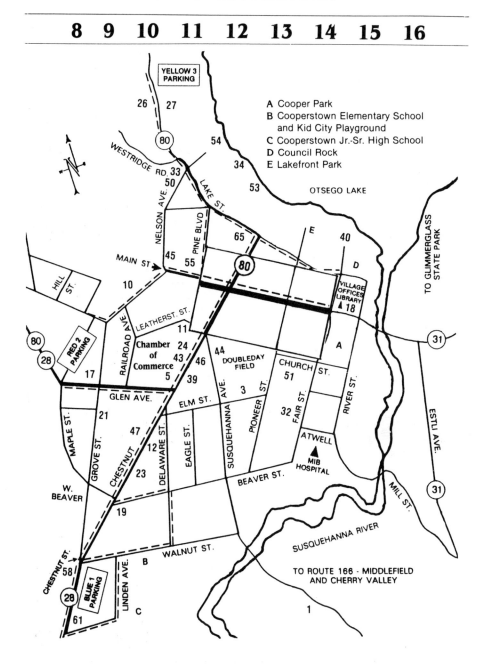

8 9 10 11 12 13 14 15 16

YELLOW 3 PARKING

A Cooper Park
B Cooperstown Elementary School and Kid City Playground
C Cooperstown Jr.-Sr. High School
D Council Rock
E Lakefront Park

OTSEGO LAKE

TO GLIMMERGLASS STATE PARK

WESTRIDGE RD.

NELSON AVE.

LAKE ST.

PINE BLVD

MAIN ST.

HILL ST.

LEATHERST. ST.

RAILROAD AVE.

Chamber of Commerce

DOUBLEDAY FIELD

CHURCH ST.

RIVER ST.

FAIR ST.

PIONEER ST.

SUSQUEHANNA AVE.

EAGLE ST.

ELM ST.

GLEN AVE.

MAPLE ST.

GROVE ST.

CHESTNUT

DELAWARE ST.

BEAVER ST.

W. BEAVER

ATWELL

MIB HOSPITAL

VILLAGE OFFICES LIBRARY

MILL ST.

ESTLI AVE.

CHESTNUT ST.

LINDEN AVE.

WALNUT ST.

BLUE 1 PARKING

RED 2 PARKING

SUSQUEHANNA RIVER

TO ROUTE 166 - MIDDLEFIELD AND CHERRY VALLEY

FIGURE D

COOPERSTOWN VILLAGE AREA

1 Alfred Corning Clark Gymnasium (L13)
2 American Sport Shop (C3)
3 Angelholm (H12)
4 Ashley-Connor Realty (C1)
5 Baseball Bed & Breakfast (G10)
6 Baseball Hall of Fame (C7)
7 Baseball Town Motel (C7)
8 Bassett House Inn (B7)
9 Beeffees Restaurant (B6)
10 Bruce Hall Corporation (E9)
11 Burrows Bed & Breakfast (F10)
12 Chestnut Street Guest House (I10)
13 Church and Scott, Inc. (C5)
14 The Colonial Agency (C2)
15 Cooper Country Crafts (D3)
16 Cooper Inn (B3)
17 Cooperstown Agway (G8)
18 Cooperstown Art Association (E14)
19 Cooperstown Motel (J9)
20 The Cupboard (C5)
21 Davidson's Jewelry (H9)
22 Doubleday Dip (D4)
23 Edward's Bed & Breakfast (I9)
24 Ellsworth House (F9)
25 The Factory Store (C4)
26 The Farmers' Museum (A9)
27 Fenimore House Museum (A10)
28 Larry Fritsch Baseball Card Museum (A2)
29 Gallery 53 (B4)
30 Glimmerglass Restaurant and B&B (B5)
31 Global Traders, Que Importa (E1)
32 Gourmet Connection Catering (C4)
33 Green Apple Inn (C10)

34 Hawkeye Bar and Grill (B12)
35 Holley Music (D5)
36 Homescapes (C3)
37 Hubbell's Real Estate (C3)
38 The Inn at Cooperstown (B2)
39 The J.P. Sill House (G11)
40 Lake Front Motel (D14)
41 Lamb Realty (B2)
42 Leather Originals (C6)
43 Lindsey House Bed & Breakfast (G10)
44 Malone Insurance (G11)
45 Main Street Bed & Breakfast (D10)
46 Miss Mae Wilbur's House (G11)
47 Mohican Motel (H10)
48 Willis Monie Books (C3)
49 Moon Dreams Shop and Tea Room (C4)
50 Nelson Avenue Pines (C10)
51 Nineteen Church Street B&B (G13)
52 Northern Catskill Dental Assoc. (D3)
53 The Otesaga Hotel (B12)
54 Otesaga Leatherstocking Golf Course (B11)
55 Overlook Bed & Breakfast (D11)
56 Pioneer Street Stadium (C6)
57 Pro Image Photo (C5)
58 The Rose & Thistle B&B (L8)
59 Sal's Pizzeria (B5)
60 Smithy/Pioneer Gallery (D6)
61 Staffin Realty (L8)
62 Tin Bin Alley (B4)
63 Toad Hall, The Shop (E6)
64 Tunnicliff Inn (B5)
65 Wynterholm (D12)

Chamber of Commerce

31 Chestnut Street

Cooperstown, NY 13326

(607) 547-9983

Relax and Enjoy

FIGURE E

180

COOPERSTOWN AREA MAPS

Chamber of Commerce
Cooperstown, NY

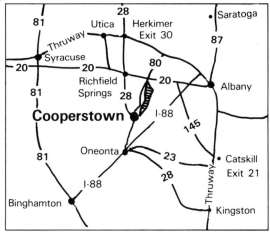

FIGURE F

How To Get Here

Cooperstown is located in central New York State, 70 miles west of Albany and 30 miles south of the New York State Thruway.

From the west or north:

Thruway Exit 30 at Herkimer, south on Rte. 28 to Cooperstown.

OR, - From Exit 30, south on Rte. 28 to Rte 20, east on 20 to Rte. 80, south to Cooperstown.

From the east or north:

Thruway Exit 25A, I-88 to Duanesburg, west on Rte. 20 to Rte. 80, south on 80.

From the south:

I-88 from Binghamton, Exit 17, Rte. 28 north to Cooperstown.

From the southeast:

Thruway Exit 21 at Catskill, Rte. 23 west, Rte. 145 north, Rte. 20 west, Rte. 80 south to Cooperstown.

OR, - Thruway Exit 21, Rte 23 west, I-88 east, Exit 17, Rte. 28 north to Cooperstown.

Pine Hills Trailways provides twice-a-day round trip bus service between Cooperstown and New York City's Port Authority Bus Terminal.

APPENDIX G:

Parking in Cooperstown

Free parking is available in three lots as follows:

(1)   Off Route 28, south of Cooperstown. Follow Walnut Street to Linden Avenue.

(2)   Off Route 28 (Glen Avenue) at Maple Street.

(3)   Route 80 north of Cooperstown at the upper parking lot of Fenimore House.

There is limited parking in the Doubleday Plaza lot and on some streets, but these areas are blocked off during the Induction weekend.

A trolley service is in operation during the Spring, Summer and Fall: A pass for $1.50 allows the visitor to ride the trolley all day.

SUMMER: June to Labour Day - 8:30 a.m. to 9:00 p.m. daily. The last trolley leaves the Hall of Fame at 9:00 p.m.

SPRING AND FALL: Memorial Day Weekend, June, September, October - 8:30 a.m. to 9:00 p.m. Weekends - 8:30 a.m. to 6:00 p.m.

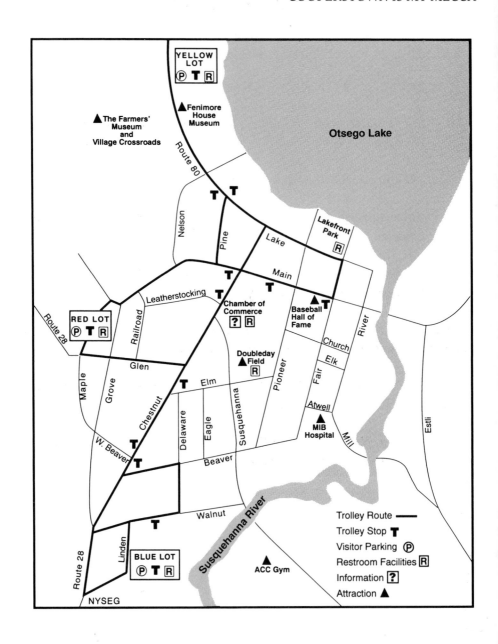

FIGURE G

184

APPENDIX H:

Members of the National Baseball Hall of Fame

1936   Tyrus R. Cobb
Walter P. Johnson
Christopher Mathewson
George H. "Babe" Ruth
John P. "Honus" Wagner

1937   Morgan G. Bulkeley
Byron B. "Ban" Johnson
Napoleon "Larry" Lajoie
Connie Mack
John J. McGraw
Tristram E. Speaker
George Wright
Denton T. "Cy" Young

1938   Grover C. Alexander
Alexander J. Cartwright, Jr.
Henry Chadwick

1939   Adrian C. "Cap" Anson
Edward T. Collins
Charles A. Comiskey
William A. "Candy"
    Cummings
William B. "Buck" Ewing
H. Louis Gehrig
William H. "Willie" Keeler
Charles G. Radbourne
George H. Sisler
Albert G. Spalding

1942   Rogers Hornsby

1944   Kenesaw M. Landis

1945   Roger P. Bresnahan

Dennis "Dan" Brouthers
Frederick C. Clarke
James J. Collins
Edward J. Delahanty
Hugh Duffy
Hugh A. Jennings
Michael J. "King" Kelly
James H. O'Rourke
Wilbert Robinson

1946   Jesse C. Burkett
Frank L. Chance
John D. Chesbro
John J. Evers
Clark C. Griffith
Thomas F. McCarthy
Joseph J. McGinnity
Edward S. Plank
Joseph B. Tinker
George E. "Rube" Waddell
Edward A. Walsh

1947   Gordon S. "Mickey"
    Cochrane
Frank F. Frisch
Robert M. "Lefty" Grove
Carl O. Hubbell

1948   Herbert J. Pennock
Harold J. "Pie" Traynor

1949   Mordecai P. Brown
Charles L. Gehringer
Charles A. "Kid" Nichols

1951   James E. Foxx

Melvin T. Ott

1952 Harry E. Heilmann
Paul G. Waner

1953 Edward G. Barrow
Charles A. "Chief" Bender
Thomas H. Connolly
Jay H. "Dizzy" Dean
William L. Klem
Aloysius H. Simmons
Roderick J. "Bobby"
   Wallace
William H. "Harry" Wright

1954 William M. Dickey
Walter J. "Rabbit"
   Maranville
William H. Terry

1955 J. Franklin Baker
   * Joseph P. DiMaggio
Charles L. "Gabby"
   Hartnett
Theodore A. Lyons
Raymond W. Schalk
Arthur C. "Dazzy" Vance

1956 Joseph H. Cronin
Henry B. Greenberg

1957 Samuel E. Crawford
Joseph V. McCarthy

1959 Zachariah D. Wheat

1961 Max G. Carey
William R. Hamilton

1962 * Robert W.A. Feller
William B. McKechnie
Jack R. Robinson
Edd J. Roush

1963 John G. Clarkson
Elmer H. Flick
Edgar C. "Sam" Rice
Eppa Rixey

1964 Lucius B. "Luke" Appling
Urban C. "Red" Faber
Burleigh A. Grimes
Miller J. Huggins
Timothy J. Keefe
Henry E. "Heinie" Manush
John M. Ward

1965 James F. "Pud" Galvin

1966 Charles D. "Casey" Stengel
   * Theodore S. Williams

1967 W. Branch Rickey
Charles H. "Red" Ruffing
Lloyd J. Waner

1968 Hazen S. "Kiki" Cuyler
Leon A. "Goose" Goslin
Joseph M. Medwick

1969 Roy Campanella
Stanley A. Coveleski
Waite C. Hoyt
   * Stanley F. Musial

1970 * Louis Boudreau
Earle B. Combs

Ford C. Frick
Jesse J. "Pop" Haines

1971
David J. Bancroft
Jacob P. Beckley
Charles J. "Chick" Hafey
Harry B. Hooper
Joseph J. Kelley
Richard W. "Rube"
   Marquard
Leory R. "Satchel" Paige
George M. Weiss

1972
* Lawrence P. "Yogi" Berra
Joshua Gibson
Vernon L. "Lefty" Gomez
William Harridge
* Sanford Koufax
* Walter F. "Buck" Leonard
* Early Wynn
Ross M. Youngs

1973
Roberto W. Clemente
William G. Evans
* Monford "Monte" Irvin
George L. Kelly
* Warren E. Spahn
Michael F. Welch

1974
James T. "Cool Papa" Bell
James L. Bottomley
John B. "Jocko" Conlan
* Edward C. "Whitey" Ford
* Mickey C. Mantle
Samuel L. Thompson

1975
H. Earl Averill
Stanley R. "Bucky" Harris

William J. Herman
William J. "Judy" Johnson
* Ralph M. Kiner

1976
Oscar M. Charleston
Roger Connor
R. Cal Hubbard
* Robert G. Lemon
Frederick C. Lindstrom
* Robin E. Roberts

1977
* Ernest Banks
Martin Dihigo
John H. Lloyd
* Alfonso R. Lopez
Amos W. Rusie
Joseph W. Sewell

1978
Adrian Joss
Leland S. "Larry" MacPhail
* Edwin L. Mathews

1979
Warren C. Giles
* Willie H. Mays
Lewis R. "Hack" Wilson

1980
* Albert W. Kaline
Charles H. Klein
* Edwin D. "Duke" Snider
Thomas A. Yawkey

1981
Andrew "Rube" Foster
* Robert Gibson
John R. Mize

1982
* Henry L. Aaron
Albert B. "Happy"
   Chandler

Travis C. "Stonewall"
   Jackson
* Frank Robinson

1983   Walter E. Alston
* George C. Kell
* Juan A. Marichal
* Brooks C. Robinson, Jr.

1984   * Luis E. Aparicio
   Donald S. Drysdale
* Richard B. Ferrell
* Harmon C. Killebrew
* Harold H. "Pee Wee" Reese

1985   * Louis C. Brock
* Enos B. "Country"
   Slaughter
   Joseph F. "Arky" Vaughan
* James Hoyt Wilhelm

1986   * Robert P. Doerr
   Ernest Lombardi
* Willie L. "Stretch"
   McCovey

1987   Raymond E. Dandridge
* James A. "Catfish" Hunter
* Billy L. Williams

1988   * Wilver D. "Willie" Stargell

1989   * Albert J. Barlick
* Johnny L. Bench
* Albert F. "Red"
   Schoendienst
* Carl M. "Yaz" Yastrzemski

1990   * Joe L. Morgan
* James A. Palmer

1991   * Rodney C. Carew
* Ferguson A. Jenkins
   Anthony M. Lazzeri
* Gaylord J. Perry
   Bill Veeck

1992   * Roland G. Fingers
   William A. McGowan
* Harold Newhouser
* George T. Seaver

1993   * Reginald M. Jackson

1994   * Steven N. Carlton
   Leo E. Durocher
* Philip F. Rizzuto

1995   * Michael Schmidt

Total Members - 220   * Living - 56

January 10, 1995

BIBLIOGRAPHY

Diaries:

The author's personal diaries from the years 1985 - 1994 inclusive.

Newspapers:

Albany Times Union, October 1, 1986
Baltimore Sun, 1993
Baltimore Evening Sun, 1993
Chicago's Sunday American, 1964
Cincinnati Post, 1985
Clearwater Sun, 1982
Columbia Daily Tribune, 1973
Dayton Daily News, 1982, 1983, 1992
Guild Reporter, 1971
Los Angeles Times, 1962, 1988
Miami Herald, 1982
New York Daily News, 1982, 1984, 1987
New York Post, 1985, 1993
New York Times, 1965, 1972, 1975, 1979 and 1980
Oneonta Daily Star, 1982, 1992, 1994
Philadelphia Enquirer, 1982, 1990
St. Louis Post - Dispatch, 1966, 1972, 1974,1975,1977,1979,1980,1989
St. Petersburg Times, 1963, 1965, 1969

Times of Trenton, 1993
Washington Post, 1982

News Releases:

American League, July 1981
Baseball Writers' Association of America, July 25, 1962
Baseball Writers' Association of America Scorebook, No 1(1962);
    No 4 (1965); No 6 (1967).
Broadcast International - on Vin Scully (no date)
Detroit Tigers, July 1, 1981
National Baseball Hall of Fame and Museum, Inc., February 1979;

February 1980; January 1984; February 1985; February 1986;
February 1988; January 1989.
National Broadcasting Service, 1990.

Periodicals:

Cooperstown Area Guide, 1986.
Hall of Fame, 53rd Annual Induction Programme, 1992
Hall of Fame, 54th Annual Induction Programme, 1993
Inside Sports, 1984.
Parade Magazine, 1988.
Sports Collectors Digest, January 1, 1993
Sporting News, March 1, 1946; May 14, 1966; November 2, 1968;
    July 4, 1970; December 12, 1970; June 22, 1974; April 26, 1975;
    September 24, 1977; October —, 1977; August 1, 1981
The Show, July 1990
United Telegraph Sunday Magazine, June 1960.

Books:

Cooper, James Fenimore. *The Deerslayer.*
    (New York: Signet Classic Books,1963)
Connor, Anthony J. *Voices from Cooperstown.*
    (New York: Collier Books, MacMillan Publishing Company, 1982).
Smith, Ken. *Baseball's Hall of Fame.*
    (New York: Tempo Books, Grosset and Dunlap, 1981)
Thorn, John, ed. *The Armchair Book of Baseball.*
    (New York: Charles Scribner's Sons, 1985).

ABOUT THE AUTHOR

Rudy Gafur emigrated to Canada from Guyana in 1972. He saw his first baseball game in 1977 when the Toronto Blue Jays played their inaugural home opener, and first visited the National Baseball Hall of Fame in 1986.

Over the years he has developed a deep love for the National Pastime, and has become a keen student of its history. His abiding passion, however, is the National Baseball Hall of Fame - his Mecca - to which he has made twelve pilgrimages in nine years.

Gafur is a member of the Toronto Blue Jays Fan Club, the "Friends of the Hall of Fame," and the Society for American Baseball Research (SABR). He resides with his family in Metropolitan Toronto.

"MY EPITAPH"

"Gone to a ballgame in a Higher League."